THE UN-DEVOTIONAL FOR TEENS

The Un-Devotional for Teens

Fun Puzzles to Help You Learn Scripture

Kathy Collard Miller

SERVANT PUBLICATIONS
ANN ARBOR, MICHIGAN

Vine Books is an imprint of Servant Publications especially designed to serve evangelical Christians.

All Scripture quotations are taken from the HOLY BIBLE, NEW INTERNATIONAL VERSION. Copyright 1973, 1978, 1984 by International Bible Society. Used by permission of Zondervan Publishing House. All rights reserved.

Servant Publications
P.O. Box 8617
Ann Arbor, MI 48107

Cover design by Alan Furst, Inc., Minneapolis, Minn.

03 04 10 9 8 7 6 5 4 3 2

Printed in the United States of America
ISBN 1-56955-250-9

Miller, Kathy C. (Kathy Collard), 1949-
    The un-devotional for teens : fun puzzles to help you learn scripture / Kathy Collard Miller.
        p. cm.
    Summary: Introduces daily devotions for teenagers through sixty word puzzles, each geared to a short passage from a different book of the Bible, plus a wrap-up to each week's theme.
    ISBN 1-56955-250-9 (alk. paper)
    1. Teenagers—Prayer-books and devotions—English. 2. Bible games and puzzles—Juvenile literature. [1. Prayer books and devotions. 2. Bible games and puzzles. 3. Word games. 4. Christian life.] I. Title.

BV4850 .M48 2001
242'.63—dc21
                                                        2001045553

Contents

Dedication

To the special "younguns" in my life—

Sara Collard
Brian Collard
Kelly Dye
Scott Collard
Megan Collard

My prayer is that you each
will grow strong in the Lord.

"Aunt" Kathy

Introduction

Let me guess. There was a time when you decided to read the Bible. You thought, "Let's see ... where do I start? Well, I guess the best place is at the beginning!"

So you began reading at Genesis but soon found the going tough. There were parts that you found hard to understand, and—yes, let's be honest—some parts were pretty boring! Before you knew it, you weren't so motivated to keep reading.

Well, you have in your hands a great new way to make the Bible come alive—The *Un-Devotional for Teens.* In a unique and wonderful way, you'll be studying the Bible—and learning—while having fun, lots of fun! Sound great? Now you've got the idea. Won't it be exciting to be able to say, "I'm studying the Bible," and yet be solving a puzzle? You'll amaze your friends—and especially your parents.

How It Works

In this book, you'll find fun and challenging puzzles for forty-five of the sixty-six books of the Bible. These forty-five puzzles can be used for daily devotions over nine weeks. Plus, there is a "Weekend Workout" to wrap up each week's theme for you to do over the weekend. Among the puzzles, you'll find four different kinds: Crossword Puzzles, Word Searches, Word Scrambles, and Word Finds.

How Do the Clues Work?

After each clue, you'll find a phrase such as "2 wds, vs 3." This will tell you how many words you are looking for, and in which verse they may be found—in this case you are looking for 2 words found in verse 3 of whatever chapter of the Bible is in the title of the puzzle. If you go to that verse of the Bible, you'll find the word or words you need. If you'd like a more difficult challenge on the Word Scrambles, cover up the verse numbers as you read the Scripture passage and solve the puzzle.

Which Bible Should I Use?

The words for the puzzles have been taken from the New International Version (NIV) of the Bible.

Need Help Looking Up Bible Verses?

If you're familiar with using the Bible, you may not need to read this section. This is primarily for those who are just starting to learn how to read God's Word. Each verse in the Bible can be found by its "address," or reference. Most of the time, a reference has three parts, and looks like this:

1 John 2:9

The first part ("1 John") tells you the *book* of the Bible in which the verse can be found. (Note: 1 John is one of the epistles, near the end of the New Testament. If you see "John" without a number in front of it, this refers to the Gospel of John, the fourth book in the New Testament.) The second part of the reference (the number before the colon—in this case, a "2") is the *chapter* within that book.

The third part (the number after the colon—in this case, a "9") is the *verse!*

ONE
To Find a Book of the Bible:

The Bible is like a library: it is made up of many books, which have been divided into two sections, the Old Testament and the New Testament. The Old Testament tells us what happened in the Jewish people's lives before Jesus came to earth. The New Testament is the story of the life of Jesus and his followers, and the story of the early Christian church.

At the beginning of every Bible is a table of contents. You can use that to find the page number of a particular book of the Bible. In most cases, the books of the Bible are listed both chronologically (in order of their appearance) and alphabetically.

Now, once you look at the table of contents, you'll see some books that have numbers in front of the titles, like 1 Chronicles and 2 Chronicles or 1 John and 2 John. That just means that there are two or three books written by the same person, so they have been numbered.

TWO
To Find a Particular Chapter:

Once you have found the book you want, then you can locate the chapter. Each book is broken into chapters. So, if you want to find the second chapter of 1 John, turn to 1 John (near the back of the Bible) and look for the big number "2" in the margin. That is the beginning of the second chapter. You can find all the chapters this way.

THREE
To Find a Particular Verse:

Each chapter is broken into verses, with each new chapter starting over again at verse 1, so it's important to make sure you have the right chapter before you try to find the verse!

Ready to Begin?

Our very first puzzle is based on the thirteenth chapter of "1 Corinthians" (also called "First Corinthians"). So you'll look up "1 Corinthians" and then you'll go to the thirteenth chapter. Beside each clue, you'll find the verse numbers for that chapter. You can try to solve the puzzle with or without looking up the passage, but be sure to read the passage either before or after you work the puzzle, so that you get that spiritual shot of blessing for your soul.

Once you start using these ideas, you will become very familiar and comfortable with it all, so don't get frustrated. Just hang in there!

I hope you enjoy this book. Please let me know if you do or if you have any questions about the Bible or God by e-mailing me at Kathy@KathyCollardMiller.com. If we publish future books like this, you could be a part of it, just like the kids who submitted ideas for this book (you'll find their names by some of the puzzles). Send me your crossword puzzles based on a short passage of the Bible and I'll let you know if they are published. Be sure to include your name, age, and address along with your submission. Send them to the address below.
Happy puzzle solving!

Kathy Collard Miller
P.O. Box 1058
Placentia, CA 92871
www.kathycollardmiller.com

Week One:

Love God With All Your Heart

Monday:
What's Love Got to Do With It?

Read 1 Corinthians 13

Thought for Today: Life isn't about who has the most dates or the biggest bouquet in her locker on Valentine's Day. Life is all about love—but not the earthly kind ... So when you go to school on February 14, hold your head high and remember, you walk on the arm of a King!

Lisa Velthouse (Brio)

Puzzle: Today it's a crossword puzzle! Look up each verse listed below to find the word you need to fill in the clue either up and down or from left to right.

1 Corinthians 13 Clues:

Across

3. This marching band instrument reminded Paul of a "brassy" person. (1 wd, vs 1)

4. Sometimes it moves mountains, sometimes it's a Hill. (1 wd, vs 2)

8. Why is love so good at school? Because love ____ ____. (2 wds, vs 8)

11. Like the Energizer Bunny with fluffy ears, true love always _____. (1 wd, vs 7)

13. Do you know someone who's always crude? That's not love; it's never _____. (1 wd, vs 5)

16. Love isn't love if it's all in the mind. Love is first of all ____ and ____. (3 wds, second word is "and," vs 4)

Down

1. After we have run the race, we will see God ____ __ ____. (3 wds, vs 12)

2. True love is based on respect: it helps, it trusts, and it _____. (1 wd, vs 7)

5. Remember: If you drop one letter and move another, it spells "DANGER!" (1 wd, vs 5)

6. Without love, they're just noise. (3 wds, vs 1)

7. I don't need a blankie or a nap these days; I have given up ____ ____. (2 wds, vs 11)

9. Love is not ___ ____; toward others it is always peeking. (1 wd, vs 5, hyphenated)

10. True love never has to ____; truth is where it wants to fly. (1 wd, vs 6)

12. A green-eyed love buster. (1 wd, vs 4)

13. Love _____ in what is right; in evil it does not delight. (1 wd, vs 6)

14. This kind of person's favorite song is "me-me-me-me-me." (1 wd, vs 4)

15. Love does not _____ in evil; to do so merely causes upheaval. (1 wd, vs 6)

Something More to Think About: Which "love quality" do you most admire in your friends? Which one bugs you most when it's missing? Write it on a note card and put it on your bedroom mirror, put it in your locker, or carry it with you, as a reminder to practice that quality today!

Rest and Restoration

Read Joel 2

Thought for Today: Every day when we wake up, that same nail-pierced hand is waiting for us. And every day we have a choice ... to go our own way or reach out and grasp the hand of Love.

Kristie Kleinow (Brio)

Puzzle: Today we have a word scramble! Look up each verse, and find a word that can be spelled using all the letters of the "scramble" just once. Write your answer in the space next to it. When you have finished the answer, transfer the letter in the box to the blanks below to answer the final question. Have fun!

Scrambled word	Solution
esnsbgil (verse 14)	_ _ _ _ _ _ _ ☐
emtpel rohcp (verse 17)	_ _ _ _ _ _ _ _ ☐ _ _ _
esvda (verse 32)	_ _ _ _ ☐
yipt (verse 18)	_ ☐ _ _
ym istrip (verse 28)	_ _ ☐ _ _ _ _ _
arign (verse 19)	_ _ _ ☐ _
rgaet gtnsih (verse 21)	_ _ _ _ _ _ _ _ _ ☐ _
ruacisog (verse 13)	_ _ _ ☐ _ _ _ _
torenrnh yamr (verse 20)	_ ☐ _ _ _ _ _ _ _ _ _ _
saiper hte anem (verse 26)	_ _ _ _ _ _ _ _ _ _ ☐ _ _ _
solsutc (verse 25)	_ _ _ _ _ ☐ _

14

treunr (verse 12)   ☐ _ _ _ _ _

edwsnro (verse 30)   _ ☐ _ _ _ _ _

dlsere (verse 16)   _ ☐ _ _ _ _

Transfer the boxed letters to find out why we can have hope.

_ _ _ / _ _ / _ _ / _ _ _ _ _ _ _

Something More to Think About: In Joel 2, the theme is hope. When we have hope, we feel rested and restored in our spirit. What are you feeling hopeful about today, and what are you feeling hopeless about? Write out one of the verses from Joel 2 on the inside of one of your school notebooks. See if you can recite it without looking before you go to bed tonight!

Wednesday:
Love Isn't Love Unless
You Give It Away

Read Hosea 11

Thought for Today: I want to show people love. I think it's a daily thing, learning to love God with all my heart and to love people. I'm going to fail a lot—and I do—but that doesn't change my desire.

Rebecca St. James, performing artist

Puzzle: Today let's go on a word search! First, solve the verse clues below. Then see how many you can find in the puzzle, looking from top to bottom, left to right, and diagonally.

Hosea 11 Clues:

1. When _____ was a child (1 wd, vs 1)
2. Out of _____ I called my son. (1 wd, vs 1)
3. They _____ to the Baals (1 wd, vs 2)
4. They _____ to images (2 wds, vs 2)
5. I led them with cords of_____ (2 wds, vs 4)
6. With _____ (3 wds, vs 4)
7. I _____ the yoke from their neck (1 wd, vs 4)
8. Will not _____ rule over them (1 wd, vs 5)
9. _____ in their cities (3 wds, vs 6)
10. Even if they call to the _____ (2 wds, vs 7)
11. All my _____ is aroused. (1 wd, vs 8)
12. The _____ among you. (2 wds, vs 9)
13. Nor devastate Ephraim _____ (1 wd, vs 9)
14. He will roar like a _____ (1 wd, vs 10)
15. The house of Israel with _____ (1 wd, vs 12)

Hosea 11

```
C A A V P R U I M I N P Q T E Q G Y T
F V M U I V M V H H C O O U T V Z W J
A P D G R X I R K B T T K R M C Y I Q
V D C V Z C A O M U L I O N I L M U I
G N O O L B V R U R E E G Y P T O Z E
H U M A N K I N D N E S S A J S F Y P
I V P U K D A A G E M O S T H I G H U
P S A S S Y R I A D Y F R H I W N Q N
O X S W O R D S W I L L F L A S H X P
W F S S H O L Y O N E O S I F B F L E
R U I Z Z X S E A C R V U P V R C I U
Y R O X U A I K D E C E I T W N U F C
F U N W J G U L Q N H O S A A Q J T M
X D O T O Z B O F S A C R I F I C E D
Z L D H P Z U Q O E D S A W L B X D O
C F G P L V E B B J L V E U A H Y D L
G G Z Z N I A G A K U I L W I P I Z V
```

Something More to Think About: God described his unconditional love (that means love that never fails) for his people in Hosea 11. Who is an example to you of unconditional love? How does he or she show this? Write this person a quick note or e-mail today explaining how much you appreciate his or her love.

Thursday:
Now That's the Way to Live

Read Matthew 5

Thought for Today: One type of ministry is not more important than another. It's a matter of being faithful to Jesus, and using the gifts and talents he gives us in the place where he puts us. We are working together for his glory!

Kim Boyce, performing artist

Puzzle: Today it's a crossword puzzle! Look up each verse listed below to find the word you need to fill in the clue either up and down or from left to right.

Matthew 5 Clues:

Across

4. If you think being _____ is being weak, give your brain a tweak. (1 wd, vs 5)
5. If you want to be the _____ of the earth, do good things on your turf. (1 wd, vs 13)
6. Let your _____ shine before all, so that they will hear God's call. (1 wd, vs 16)
7. Blessed are those who are _____; for theirs is the kingdom of heaven. (1 wd, vs 10)
8. _____ is a five-letter word for showing someone you care. (1 wd, vs 7)
9. If you're a Christian, _____ your light; do not pick a fight. (1 wd, vs 16)
10. Blessed are those who are _____ __ _____. The kingdom will be theirs, so do not fear it. (3 wds, vs 3)
11. When you're misunderstood, it's hard to _____, but believe me, it is still the right choice. (1 wd, vs 12)
13. Jesus had a lot to say when he saw the _____. The people heard wonderful words under the clouds. (1 wd, vs 1)

Down

1. Be a _____, not an oath breaker. (1 wd, vs 9)
2. If you ____ __ ____ for righteousness, you will be filled above the rest. (3 wds, vs 6)
3. The _____ were persecuted, so you're in good company when your friend turns on you because you say salvation is free. (1 wd, vs 12)
4. Jesus will comfort those who ___; all your sorrows will be borne. (1 wd, vs 4)
5. We don't want to lose our _____. It's our way of giving out heaven's address. (1 wd, vs 13)
10. Blessed are the ____ in heart for they will see God from the start. (1 wd, vs 8)
12. Be bold in witnessing to Jesus' love. Take the _____ off your lamp and point to heaven above. (1 wd, vs 15)

Something More to Think About: Loving means reaching out to others with the gifts God has put inside you. Today we read the qualities of a full heart Jesus talked about in Matthew 5. Which ones are naturally in you, and how do you reach out in love to others with them? Write a little prayer to God thanking him for his gift to you of these qualities.

Friday:
Stay in Tune

Read Song of Solomon (Song of Songs) 5

Thought for Today: Forget impressing someone by acting like someone you're not. Sooner or later others will find out the real you—and that's what you want them to see anyway. If a relationship is really gonna work, it's because you're completely honest with each other and completely yourself.

Tammy Trent, performing artist

Puzzle: Today we have a word scramble! Look up each verse, and find a word that can be spelled using all the letters of the "scramble" just once. Write your answer in the space next to it. When you have finished the answer, transfer the letter in the box to the blanks below to answer the final question. Have fun!

Scrambled word	Solution
rymrh (verse 1)	_ ☐ _ _ _
eosvd (verse 12)	_ ☐ _ _ _
odpnu (verse 4)	_ _ ☐ _ _
pasirpesh (verse 14)	_ _ _ _ _ ☐ _ _
guthedras (verse 8)	_ _ ☐ _ _ _ _ _
daregn (verse 1)	_ _ _ _ _ ☐
yohocmebn (verse 1)	_ _ _ _ _ ☐ _ _ _
rvyoi (verse 14)	_ _ ☐ _ _
catmhnew (verse 7)	_ _ _ _ _ _ _ ☐
debir (verse 1)	_ _ _ ☐ _
irkdn ouyr ilfl (verse 1)	_ _ _ _ _ _ _ _ _ _ _ ☐ _ _

20

terah (verse 2)   _ _ _ _ ☐

prddpie (verse 5)   _ _ ☐ _ _ _ _

kolac (verse 7)   _ _ ☐ _ _

nealnob (verse 15)   _ _ _ _ ☐ _ _

saewhd (verse 3)   _ ☐ _ _ _ _

levdoeb (verse 9)   _ _ ☐ _ _ _ _

shlenad (verse 5)   _ _ _ _ ☐ _ _

liopdehs (verse 14)   _ ☐ _ _ _ _ _ _

olvyel (verse 16)   _ _ ☐ _ _ _

efrupem (verse 13)   _ _ _ _ _ _ ☐

Transfer the boxed letters to find out what other people will like best about you.

_ _ _ _ / _ _ _ _ _ _ _ _ _ _ _ _ _ _ _ / _ _ _ _

Something More to Think About: When do you find yourself trying to act like something or someone you're not? Why do you think this happens? Think about one thing you like about yourself and focus on that all day today. Remember at least five times today how much God loves you—just as you are!

Weekend Workout:
Give Love Freely

This "workout" has two parts!

Create a prayer journal. A prayer journal is a book in which you can record your prayer requests and other thoughts you have about God and about being a Christian. You can decorate your notebook with pictures of friends and family, or write a prayer-poem to God on the front cover. In one section, write the things you have requested from God, for yourself or for other people. Don't forget to leave a space for the answers!

Let Jesus love others through you. Choose one of the ideas below—or come up with one of your own! If anyone asks why you're doing what you're doing, tell that person it's a reminder that God loves him (or her). Don't forget to write a prayer to God in your journal, telling him about the experience.

- Bake a batch of cookies and share them with your next-door neighbor. As you talk with him or her, find out what's going on in his or her life, and remember to pray for that family at least once during the weekend.

- Do a chore your mom or dad dislikes—do the dishes, mow the lawn, or clean the bathroom. Don't tell them about it ... let them be surprised! As you work, don't forget to use the time to pray for your own family's needs.

- Spend an hour with a younger sibling, doing what he or she wants to do. If you don't have a younger brother or sister, entertain your neighbor's kid! Find out what's going on in his or her life, and don't forget to pray!

Week Two:

Generosity Always Pays

Monday:
Don't Rob God, It Doesn't Pay

Read Malachi 3

Thought for Today: Stewardship means that God owns everything. He gives us things to look after (to manage). Since everything belongs to God, we need to take care of what we have the way he tells us to in the Bible. When we do that, we can trust God to take care of us.

Larry Burkett, financial expert

Puzzle: Today let's go on a word search! First, solve the verse clues below. Then see how many you can find in the puzzle, looking from top to bottom, left to right, and diagonally.

Malachi 3 Clues:

1. I will send my messenger, who will _____ before me (3 wds, vs 1)
2. But who can endure the _____ (4 wds, vs 2)
3. He will sit as a _____ and purifier of silver (1 wd, vs 3)
4. The offerings of Judah and Jerusalem will be _____ to the Lord (1 wd, vs 4)
5. So I will _____ near to you for judgment (1 wd, vs 5)
6. I the Lord _____ (3 wds, vs 6)
7. Will a man _____ God? (1 wd, vs 8)
8. But you ask, "How do we rob you?" "In _____ and offerings" (1 wd, vs 8)
9. Bring the whole tithe into the _____ (1 wd, vs 10)
10. I will prevent _____ from devouring your crops (1 wd, vs 11)
11. For yours will be a _____ (2 wds, vs 12)
12. You have said, "It is futile to _____ God" (1 wd, vs 14)
13. A scroll of _____ was written in his presence (1 wd, vs 16)
14. In the day when I make up my _____ (2 wds, vs 17)
15. You will again see the distinction between the _____ and the wicked (1 wd, vs 18)

Malachi 3

```
U X E B H Y T I Z Q C B S L Z J N Z X
J N K G Z P D L C X U O E L X Z F A S
U Q N C T M T B R T N T M X O D P A G
C I B W X Z Z J Y I V I R D P V B K P
D L J N N Z W T C J G T F D C Z T F M
L E L V V P G G R J P H C X Y O W N S
G F D A A V R N N S M E T J F F V K T
T R E A S U R E D P O S S E S S I O N
E S L I Y N E E P Q P L K T O Q W T C
F Q I M I O H R M A G I C U S U M H Y
C D G Q R E F I N E R K D W X G S P H
U L H Q Y G P H C M M E M F P E F H F
T I T Y N L R W I A P B T N S H H G P
E I F I C K I Z Y S A Y R H O R Z Y X
W X U H P A J L G I C X L A E C L D J
J B L G I P N F U K C O M E N W E U G
D U L H E R Z Y P D E F M B C C A B I
I C A C M I K E H R P O K I W D E Y L
Z D N X I K D O N O T C H A N G E H C
E Z D J E S F U O V A Z Q T L G Y C D
P J H J G O Z B R O B Y D V M B J E R
C E E I N Z L C V J L T K K T H R N G
J S T O R E H O U S E R V E Y Z C I U
```

Something More to Think About: Why do you think God wants us to give some of our money back to him? Write in your prayer journal about it. If you have never given a "tithe" (which means 10 percent) to God, maybe today is a good day to start! If you can't give money, how about giving God a share of your time?

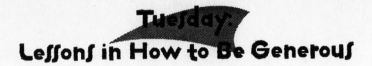

Tuesday:
Lessons in How to Be Generous

Read 2 Corinthians 9

Thought for Today: When I was a teenager, the most popular business advertisements in magazines read: SEND ME A MAN WHO READS. As much as I value reading and applaud the resourcefulness of those who pore over the pages of good books, I think today's slogan should be: SEND ME ONE WHOSE ATTITUDE IS POSITIVE, WHOSE HEART IS FULL OF CHEER, WHOSE FACE SHOUTS YES!

Charles Swindoll, pastor and writer

2 Corinthians 9 Clues:

Across

1. When you give to a foreign mission, you are God's tool. You are _____ of God's people and that's very cool. (3 wds, vs 12)

3. God has given Jesus, his _____. We can't match it, but let's not be spendthrift. (2 wds, vs 15)

5. You should give cheerfully what is in your _____ to give, and God will make sure you have what you need to live. (1 wd, vs 7)

7. Regardless of whether you have lots or little, God considers you _____— his gifts don't belittle. (4 wds, vs 11)

9. Whoever plants _____ in the lives of others will also receive _____ from God's hand. (same 1 wd, vs 6)

12. __ ___ will result in thanksgiving; through God you will abound in every good thing. (2 wds, vs 11)

13. _____ you will abound; as you give generously riches will be found. (4 wds, vs 8)

15. In everything you will ___; when you share what you have, happiness will be found. (1 wd, vs 8)

Down

2. God has _____ _____ his gifts to the poor; it is he who supplies seed to the sower. (2 wds, vs 9)

4. Whoever gives _____ will also receive _____. (same 1 wd, vs 6)

6. God loves a _____, so don't be stingy, share with others. (2 wds, vs 7)

7. Don't give _____ to the church offering. Put your money in, then joyfully sing. (1 wd, vs 7)

8. If you want to know whether _____ _____ of faith is real, put it to the test by giving with zeal. (2 wds, vs 13)
10. Since God knows what _____, he will provide. From worry you are freed! (2 wds, vs 8)
11. Your harvest of righteousness God will _____; there's no need to worry when God's in charge. (1 wd, vs 10)
14. Others will thank _____ because of your deeds; give and he will supply all your needs. (1 wd, vs 11)

Wednesday:
Be Wealthy but Be Wise

Read Ecclesiastes 5

Thought for Today: Attention and money are great, but they don't offer you a lot. Worldly things are not the answer.... Once you realize the satisfaction from pleasing God, you won't worry about trying to please the world. Then he can make your way truly prosperous and successful.

David Robinson, professional basketball player

Puzzle: Today we have a word scramble! Look up each verse, and find a word that can be spelled using all the letters of the "scramble" just once. When you have finished the answer, transfer the letter in the box to the blanks below to answer the final question. Have fun!

Scrambled word	Solution
lsoti (verse 16)	_ _ □ _ _
elnits (verse 1)	_ _ _ □ _ _
asnticastiof (verse 18)	_ _ _ _ _ _ _ _ □ _
sperulea (verse 4)	_ _ _ _ □ _ _ _
nardigem (verse 7)	_ _ _ _ _ _ □ _
rudga uoyr etssp (verse 1)	_ _ _ _ _ _ _ _ _ _ _ □ _
avhene (verse 2)	_ _ _ □ _ _
epshec (verse 3)	_ _ □ _ _ _
ihcr amn (verse 12)	□ _ _ _ _ _ _
ebntfie (verse 11)	_ □ _ _ _ _ _

28

enmyo (verse 10) `_ _ □ _ _`

erptots (verse 6) `_ _ □ _ _ _ _`

tisumfrnoe
(verse 14) `_ _ _ _ _ _ _ □ _ _`

sadgnles fo taerh `□ _ _ _ _ _ _ _ _ _ _ _ _ _ _ _`
(verse 20)

letwah (verse 10) `_ _ _ _ _ □`

Transfer the boxed letters to find out why money can't satisfy.

`_ _ / _ _ / _ _ _ _ _ / _ _ _ _ _ _`

Something More to Think About: Think about something that you wanted to have for a long time. When you got it, how long were you satisfied? An hour? A day? Longer? Write a prayer to God in your journal, thanking him for giving you the things you need most—especially a relationship with him!

Thursday:
Rebuilding the Wall

Read Haggai 1

Thought for Today: I had one of those worship books with the guitar chords.... I figured that if I could memorize where my left hand needed to be, I could concentrate on the worship aspect and let the guitar sorta take care of itself. God increases whatever talents you use for him.

Eli (Elijah Stone), Christian performing artist

Puzzle: Today it's a crossword puzzle! Look up each verse listed below to find the word you need to fill in the clue either up and down or from left to right.

Haggai 1 Clues:

Across

2. Everyone began working on the house of the _____; in God's service they were never bored. (1 wd, vs 14)
3. Because the people away from God had turned, the heaven held back the _____ and with drought the crops were burned. (1 wd, vs 10)
5. I'll give you a clue, they're up near the blue. (1 wd, vs 8)
7. First the people obeyed and then they were _____. (1 wd, vs 12)
9. What is slippery, is used in cars, and rhymes with toil? (1 wd, vs 11)
11. _____ gave the message of the Lord, for which he should have been given an award. (1 wd, vs 13)
12. What remains a ruin? (1 wd, vs 9)
13. Garments in our wardrobe are called _____. (1 wd, vs 6)

Down

1. Without any rain, the ground didn't produce any _____. (1 wd, vs 11)
4. The Lord said, "In all your days give careful thought to your _____." (1 wd, vs 7)
6. This is another name for God's Chosen People, who (hint) live in Israel. (1 wd)
7. "Build my house," the Lord ____ says, and I will reward you for the rest of your days. (1 wd, vs 7)
8. In anger God called for a ____ to drive the people's indifference out. (1 wd, vs 11)
10. A _____ isn't supposed to have holes, yet sometimes that describes people's souls. (1 wd, vs 6)

[*Puzzle created by Carol Burlew's Sunday school class:*
Rene Marquez, Paul Rogers Jr., David Roman, and Jordan Turner]

Something More to Think About: God used Haggai's talents to lead the people. Do you consider yourself a follower or a leader? If you're a follower, are you following those who will lead you closer to God? If you're a leader, are you leading your friends closer to God? Write in your journal about one way that you are doing each of these things.

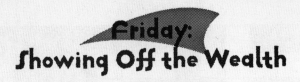

Showing Off the Wealth

Read 2 Chronicles 9

Thought for Today: We come into the world with nothing, and we leave the world with nothing. Whatever we have to use in the interim belongs to God, whether it is a little or a lot.

Ron and Judy Blue

Puzzle: Today we have a word scramble! Look up each verse, and find a word that can be spelled using all the letters of the "scramble" just once. Write your answer in the space next to it. When you have finished the answer, transfer the letter in the box to the blanks below to answer the final question.

Scrambled word	Solution
hedlidteg (verse 8)	_ _ _ _ ☐ _ _ _ _
lnomoso (verse 1)	_ _ _ ☐ _ _ _
dimn (verse 1)	_ _ _ ☐
dolg (verse 10)	☐ _ _ _
ipares (verse 8)	_ _ _ ☐ _ _
gnidnatet enstrvas (verse 4)	_ _ _ _ _ _ _ _ _ _ _ ☐ _ _ _
tntlsea (verse 9)	_ _ _ ☐ _ _ _
cseisp (verse 9)	_ _ _ _ _ ☐
dimows (verse 3)	☐ _ _ _ _ _
letpem (verse 11)	_ _ _ _ _ ☐
rabcerspeu (verse 4)	_ _ _ _ _ ☐ _ _ _
capale (verse 3)	_ _ ☐ _ _ _

ienustoqs (verse 2)   _ _ _ _□ _ _ _ _

uneqe fo hebsa(verse 1)   _ _ _ _ _ _ _ _□ _ _ _

Transfer the boxed letters to find out how you can resist being jealous of those who have money.

_ _ _ / _ _ _ _ _ _ / _ _ _ _ _ _

Something More to Think About: If God gives you a lot of money when you're grown up, how would you like to use it for God and his glory? If he doesn't, how do you plan to be happy, regardless of your circumstances?

Weekend Workout:
Be Generous, It Won't Hurt

At church on Sunday, give a tithe from your allowance, or if you don't receive an allowance, do an extra chore for your parents, a neighbor, or a friend so that you can earn some extra money. Typically a tithe is 10 percent of the money you receive. If this seems just too hard, start small, with 5 percent, with the goal of building up to 10 percent over the next few weeks.

Write in your journal any fears you have about giving money to God, and then record how it felt when you gave.

Extra Idea: Memorize one of the Scripture verses from this past week about giving money to God.

Week Three:

Friendfhipf Make Me Smile—Or Drive Me Crazy!

Monday: Loyalty to the Extreme

Read Ruth 1

Thought for Today: If a friend disappoints you, goes off the deep end, does something stupid, or even repulsive, that friend is still your friend. You do not say, "I'll never trust you or like you again." You're always ready to forgive and start over with a friend.

Michael W. Smith, performing artist

Puzzle: Today we have a word scramble! Look up each verse, and find a word that can be spelled using all the letters of the "scramble" just once. Write your answer in the space next to it. When you have finished the answer, transfer the letter in the box to the blanks below to answer the final question. Have fun!

Scrambled word	Solution
thebemhle (verse 2)	☐ _ _ _ _ _ _ _
egusjd (verse 1)	_ _ _ _ ☐ _
rundearmi (verse 13)	_ _ _ _ _ _ ☐ _ _
danl fo duahj (verse 7)	_ _ ☐ _ _ _ _ _ _ _ _
viprodgin odfo (verse 6)	_ _ _ _ _ _ _ _ ☐ _ _ _ _
ster (verse 9)	_ _ _ ☐
sbausnhd (verse 11)	☐ _ _ _ _ _ _ _
hows dneskins (verse 8)	_ _ _ _ _ _ _ _ _ ☐ _ _
harop (verse 4)	_ ☐ _ _ _
ptew dolua (verse 9)	_ ☐ _ _ _ _ _ _ _

Transfer the boxed letters to find a definition of real friendship.

_ _ _ _ _ / _ _ _ _ _

Something More to Think About: As you read the story about Ruth and Naomi, what bugged you about Naomi's attitude? What did you find wonderful about Ruth's attitude? Is there someone in your life who is like Naomi (maybe even you, sometimes)? If you're feeling discouraged about your friend's attitude, be sure to talk to an adult about the situation in order to gain some ideas.

The Great Way to Live

Read Romans 12

Thought for Today: It's not always easy to have our faults pointed out. But a true friend is someone who's willing to point them out in a loving way. They want you to be the best you can be.

Jaci Velasquez, performing artist

Puzzle: Today it's a crossword puzzle! Look up each verse listed below to find the word you need to fill in the clue either up and down or from left to right.

Something More to Think About: Being "accountable" to someone means asking for his or her opinion about how we're doing in some area. Do you have someone who is holding you "accountable"? It could be your youth worker, a parent, or a friend. Are there areas in which you might like some help in staying on track? Maybe with your homework? With sports activities? Having someone to cheer you on will be great! Ask God to guide you to the right person for you.

Romans 12 Clues:

Across

4. _____ means I give to others, joyfully aiding my sisters and brothers. (1 wd, vs 7)

6. I'm one of _____ in God's family, each one connected like branches on a tree. (2 wds, vs 4)

7. _____ may seem sweet at the time, but it leaves a bitter taste—like lime. (1 wd, vs 19)

8. Sacrifice isn't a fun word, but it's the way to truly _____ God. (1 wd, vs 1)

10. Even when trials take me to the end of my rope, God's power will help me be _____. (3 wds, vs 12)

11. _____ is _____ and bad is bad, don't mix them up or God will be sad. (same 1 wd, vs 9)

15. We're all unique in God's body, so we _____ differently. (1 wd, vs 4)

16. ____ diligently when needed, and in God's plan you will have succeeded. (1 wd, vs 8)

18. Don't let _____ make you sin, because only good will help you win. (1 wd, vs 21)

19. Practice ____, share with those in need. God will reward you for every good deed. (1 wd, vs 13)

22. To the patterns of the world I will not ____; I will follow God's laws though it may not be the norm. (1 wd, vs 2)

23. In _____ don't get discouraged. Govern diligently and be encouraged. (1 wd, vs 8)

24. You will heap _____ on your enemy's head if you make sure that when he's hungry he's fed. (2 wds, vs 20)

Down

1. _____—what is that? It's seeing ourselves through God's eyes and that's a fact! (2 wds, vs 3)

2. Live at ____ with all on earth; recognize each person's worth. (1 wd, vs 18)

3. _____ generously as you are able, and you will be blessed when you come to God's table. (1 wd, vs 8)

5. God gives different gifts, according to his grace from on high; with a measure of faith we can even _____. (1 wd, vs 6)

6. When practicing ____ do so with cheer, to your brothers and sisters in kindness draw near. (1 wd, vs 8)

9. _____ my mind is what I do when I study God's Word and find it's true. (1 wd, vs 2)

12. For each member, God has many different _____, so that we won't have strife and rifts. (1 wd, vs 6)

13. I'm not going to think I'm better than anyone because that's being _____ and that's no fun. (1 wd, vs 16)

38

14. _____ is just another way to say, put others first in every way. (2 wds, vs 10)
17. Doing what is _____ to my fellow man helps me see the best in others and follow God's plan. (1 wd, vs 17)
20. _____ should be sincere; be devoted, without fear. (1 wd, vs 9)
21. _____ is a noble thing. It builds up others for the purposes of the King. (1 wd, vs 7)

Wednesday:
Convincing Words

Philemon 1

Thought for Today: Relationships are America's most precious resource. Take our oil, take our weapons, but don't take what holds us together—relationships. A nation's strength is measured by the premium it puts on its own people. When people value people, an impenetrable web is drawn, a web of vitality and security.

Max Lucado, pastor and author

Puzzle: Today let's go on a word search! First, solve the verse clues below. Then see how many you can find in the puzzle, looking from top to bottom, left to right, and diagonally.

Philemon 1 Clues:

1. _____, a prisoner of Christ Jesus (1 wd, vs 1)
2. To _____ our dear friend and fellow worker (1 wd, vs 1)
3. _____ to you and peace from God our Father (1 wd, vs 3)
4. I always _____ as I remember you in my prayers (3 wds, vs 4)
5. I _____ that you may be active in sharing your faith (1 wd, vs 6)
6. Your _____ has given me great joy and encouragement (1 wd, vs 7)
7. Yet I _____ to you on the basis of love (1 wd, vs 9)
8. I then, as Paul—an old man and now also a _____ of Christ Jesus (1 wd, vs 9)
9. I am sending him—who is my very _____—back to you (1 wd, vs 12)
10. No longer as a _____ (1 wd, vs 16)
11. As a _____ in the Lord (1 wd, vs 16)

Philemon 1

```
D N I A H O C I J E L T O E
Q A J P P L S G A Q B H G H
T C J P A B C N E G R A C E
L I K E C F K A P C K N C F
U P R A Y E D M R F B K D D
M A G L F D P H I L E M O N
R U C G H C F B S I N Y P B
S L A V E H P A O L H G H M
D O J B A R C J N Q L O V E
N I B B R O T H E R D D A K
E A E M T P I K R L B J O D
```

Something More to Think About: How would you define a good friend? A bad friend? Make two columns in your journal and write down in the left column the characteristics of a good friend. In the right column, write down what a bad friend is like. Which of your friends are like the left column? Let them know today you appreciate them as friends. If any of the qualities in the right column apply to you, ask God to help you be a better friend today.

Thursday:
Jesus Is Telling Stories Again

Read Mark 4

Thought for Today: We don't know for certain if angels are doing hand-to-hand combat with demons, but we have learned from our pasts that trying to live a godly life alone is like going up against a well-equipped warrior while armed with a butter knife.

Greg Johnson, youth writer

Puzzle: Today it's a crossword puzzle! Look up each verse listed below to find the word you need to fill in the clue either up and down or from left to right.

Mark 4 Clues:

Across

1. Some _____ are like seed when they hear God's Good News. They can receive it gladly as filled with truths. (1 wd, vs 15)

4. Jesus explained that the _____ sows the word. The disciples were listening, reassured. (1 wd, vs 14)

7. On ready soil, a good crop can be grown—thirty, sixty, or even a ____ times what was sown. (1 wd, vs 8)

9. Seeds among _____ might start to grow, but soon they're choked—what a blow. (1 wd, vs 7)

11. Too many people wanted to be near. So Jesus got into a _____ and spoke loud and clear. (1 wd, vs 1)

13. Roots with _____ soil will wither when the sun comes up and they die quicker. (1 wd, vs 5)

14. The people had come to hear Jesus at _____, because their hearts were filled with ache. (2 wds, vs 1)

Down

1. By ____ Christ spread the word, so his message might be heard. (1 wd, vs 2)

2. Seeds on a _____ can be eaten, and in this way God's Word by Satan is beaten. (1 wd, vs 4)

3. _____ is what seeds love, a match that's like a hand in a glove. (2 wds, vs 8)

5. _____ don't have much soil, so seeds don't do well, no matter how much you toil. (2 wds, vs 5)

6. Whether your crop is huge or little, make sure that you are not _____. (1 wd, vs 19)

8. _____ or persecution cause some to fall away. Don't be like them, hang in there every day. (1 wd, vs 17)

10. Be like ____ on good soil. Read the Bible and commit to be loyal. (2 wds, vs 20)

12. _____ wants to take away the Word. He can't stand for people to be spiritually matured. (1 wd, vs 15)

13. Many were farmers, feeding others in need, so they understood a story about _____. (1 wd, vs 3)

Something More to Think About: Think of each of the seeds in Jesus' story. Which seed are you like right now? Which one do you want to be like? Can you see any ways that Satan, the devil, is trying to pluck your faith out of God's field? If so, what will you do about it?

Friday:
There's Always Hope With God

Read Zephaniah 3

Thought for Today: People don't remember that your teenage years are your years of meeting people and discovering yourself through that. People think that in order to find out who they are, they have to have a guy or a girl.

Rachel Lampa, recording artist

Puzzle: Today let's go on a word search! First, solve the verse clues below. Then see how many you can find in the puzzle, looking from top to bottom, left to right, and diagonally.

Zephaniah 3 Clues:

1. Woe to the _____, rebellious and defiled! (3 wds, vs 1)
2. She does not _____, she does not draw near to her God. (4 wds, vs 2)
3. Her officials are roaring _____(1 wd, vs 3)
4. Her prophets are _____ (1 wd, vs 4)
5. The Lord within her is righteous; he _____ (3 wds, vs 5)
6. I have _____ off nations (1 wd, vs 6)
7. I said to the _____, "Surely you will fear me" (1 wd, vs 7)
8. The whole world will be consumed by the _____ of my jealous anger (1 wd, vs 8)
9. Then will I _____ of the peoples (3 wds, vs 9)
10. I will remove from this city those who rejoice in their _____ (1 wd, vs 11)
11. But I will leave within you the _____ and humble (1 wd, vs 12)
12. The remnant of Israel will do no wrong; they will _____ (3 wds, vs 13)
13. Sing, O Daughter of Zion; _____ (4 wds, vs 14)
14. The Lord your God is with you, he is _____ to save (1 wd, vs 17)
15. I will _____ the lame and gather those who have been scattered (1 wd, vs 19)
16. I will give you honor and praise among all the peoples of the earth when I _____ your fortunes before your very eyes (1 wd, vs 20)

44

```
Y R Y V P J P S G S M U O A G U P V N
Q Q H C U T D X O D E Q T A L L U N U
N F H F I R E S T O R E S C U E R G O
F V U U B U R F I J D H G Q P R I D E
M Y B C Q S G L R J D Y X J A W F B Z
B F N I T T H A L F F A J H O X Y J R
A P I T G I C P L I H R M I G H T Y T
X F M Y J N K D I L Y R X I Y W H L I
X S H O U T A L O U D O I S R A E L I
M Z G F H H N F N C O G C E Z M L V D
D G L O M E E K S P E A K N O L I E S
C C D P P L A M R P S N T E B R P L M
T B C P E O L A W Y N T O C K A S A B
E R Z R P R M E B K O R U J I S B S Y
K V U E J D K L I I W E R W Z S K Q O
B E E S O L E G B O R W A G A Y E Z G
C E P S H I E X B L O R P Y Q Q T X K
U B Z O B W C G M V N J A T E R X M E
I J Q R K L O G I P G W B I N V N C E
S Y B S Z S J V N F F D N C Q L P X K
```

Something More to Think About: You can have great hope about your future and whether God wants you to be married. You can even pray for that future best friend who will be your husband or wife. In your journal, write down the qualities you'd like to find in your future spouse, and then write out a prayer for that person—even though you don't know who he or she is.

Weekend Workout:
Be the Better Friend

Friendships can be hard at times, but they can also be extreme fun! Either way, friendships take work. Consider one of these ideas for working on friendships this weekend.

- Call up someone who used to be a friend, until something happened between you. If you've been missing spending time with that person, take a risk and give him or her a call. Maybe he or she would like to hang out a bit.

- Phone a person from school whom you've never hung out with before and invite him or her to go shopping or do some activity together. You might even consider someone who isn't well liked or who is into different activities than you are. Show this person God's love by asking about his or her life—not just talking about yourself.

- Think of one of your favorite friends and plan a surprise for him or her. Maybe you could gather a bouquet of flowers from your garden—with your mom's permission, of course—and deliver it in person, or put it on the porch as an anonymous surprise. You could also send this person a card that expresses how you feel about your friendship, or you could help him or her to do some chore that needs to be done.

Be sure to pray for your friend when you choose one of these options. Write out a prayer for your friend in your journal.

Week Four:

I Can't Wait for the Future

Monday:
Look at What's Comin'

Read Revelation 21

Thought for Today: The feeling of winning Olympic gold ... it will be gone in a week. But when you look at what God has to offer—an eternity of winning the "gold" and that excitement—you see how God's reward is exceedingly greater than any honor the world can give.

Dan Russell, Olympic wrestling champion

Puzzle: Today let's go on a word search! First, solve the verse clues listed on the next page. Then see how many you can find in the puzzle, looking from top to bottom, left to right, and diagonally.

Revelation 21 Clues:

1. Then I saw a _____ and a new earth (2 wds, vs 1)
2. I saw the Holy City, the _____ (2 wds, vs 2)
3. He will _____ with them (1 wd, vs 3)
4. He will _____ every tear from their eyes (1 wd, vs 4)
5. He who was seated on the _____ (1 wd, vs 5)
6. I am the _____, the Beginning and the End (4 wds, vs 6)
7. He who _____ will inherit all this (1 wd, vs 7)
8. Their place will be in the _____ of burning sulfur (2 wds, vs 8)
9. One of the _____ angels who had the _____ bowls (same 1 wd, vs 9)
10. It shone with the _____ of God (1 wd, vs 11)
11. It had a great, high wall with twelve gates, and with _____ at the gates
    (2 wds, vs 12)
12. There were three _____ on the east (1 wd, vs 13)
13. On them were the names of the twelve apostles of the _____ (1 wd, vs 14)
14. The angel who talked with me had a _____ of gold to measure the city
    (2 wds, vs 15)
15. The city was laid out like a _____, as long as it was wide (1 wd, vs 16)
16. He measured its wall and it was 144 _____ thick (1 wd, vs 17)
17. The _____ of the city walls were decorated with every kind of precious stone
    (1 wd, vs 19)
18. I did not see a _____ in the city (1 wd, vs 22)
19. The glory and honor of the _____ will be brought into it (1 wd, vs 26)
20. Nothing _____ will ever enter it (1 wd, vs 27)

Revelation 21

```
Q K E D K Z A G U E B I W Q H K Q S M
J U V S W C B D H Z T E M P L E N E Z
L H X H Q G S W Q M G F A P I W E K Q
K J L E X Y J O M O D Q I G U M W B M
H L A T W E L V E A N G E L S R H G U
S F M L I J O G A T E S M O A V E E I
M M B Z P A N Q S V F I E R Y L A K E
E U L G E H A V U Q O K I Y M U V E N
A C A E V I A E R H U C L W R S E C W
T J D I V O D A I Q N A B F B C N S J
J I Y Z K W C D N K D C R D E W W L K
Y I H I U K E U G D A F Q E C J G V D
V T R V P N Z S R N T V J C G X K W H
O Z A K C Y T R O Z I H G P V E U K K
A T N Z V S E G D Y O V E R C O M E S
B A A A U U G Z F S N V S O X N M Q E
O D I N E W J E R U S A L E M S T Z R
Q H Q X X G S B Z V R I T I E R R Z
Q Q L I P J O V B U X Y W I V V G Y W
B M J F S N X S A F I O D F O E I A Q
B L E P L X J A T G F T H R O N E H B
R A R U Z G O L S A O C U B I T S N U
```

Something More to Think About: Someday you'll wear a crown as you stand before God's throne. In your journal, draw a picture of what you'd like your crown to look like. If you are getting together with a group of friends soon, have everyone draw a picture of their heavenly crowns. Then together share your feelings about what you'll think when you throw your crown down at Jesus' feet, in his honor. Revelation 4:10 says that this will happen.

Tuesday:
Looking Back and Looking Forward

Read Titus 3

Thought for Today: Have a firm foundation in the Word of God, to know that no matter what the world says, we have Jesus Christ on our side. Nobody can take that away. If you can stand on that fact alone, everything else will fall into place. He always gives you hope.

Leah Amico, Olympic softball champion

Puzzle: Today it's a crossword puzzle! Look up each verse listed below to find the word you need to fill in the clue either up and down or from left to right.

Titus 3 Clues:

Across

2. God says to avoid wrong passions and _____. By obedience to this we will earn heaven's treasures. (1 wd, vs 3)
4. Be sure to do _____ in everything you do; in this the love of God will shine through. (1 wd, vs 8)
6. Be _____ to those around you. Then goodwill will surround you. (1 wd, vs 2)
8. It's hard to be selfless and _____. But reach out to others, even the misfit. (1 wd, vs 2)
11. _____ is an attitude of ingratitude. (1 wd, vs 3)
12. _____ are leaders by another name; God asks us to obey them, just the same. (1 wd, vs 1)
16. You have eternal life in a heavenly place, if Jesus is in your heart through _____. (1 wd, vs 7)
17. We may not always like these, but they are necessary: _____ (1 wd, vs 1)
18. When we don't feel loved by God, we start _____ one another. Let's get smart and pass his love on to each other. (1 wd, vs 3)

Down

1. When we feel insecure we try to get our own way. But being _____ won't look good on a resume. (1 wd, vs 3)
3. Don't _____; it's not fun. That's saying something not true about someone. (1 wd, vs 2)
5. If you have God's wisdom received, then you won't find yourself _____. (1 wd, vs 3)

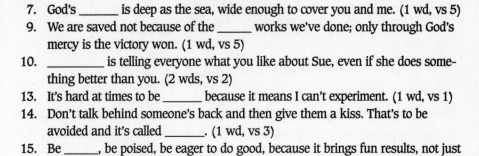

7. God's _____ is deep as the sea, wide enough to cover you and me. (1 wd, vs 5)

9. We are saved not because of the _____ works we've done; only through God's mercy is the victory won. (1 wd, vs 5)

10. _____ is telling everyone what you like about Sue, even if she does something better than you. (2 wds, vs 2)

13. It's hard at times to be _____ because it means I can't experiment. (1 wd, vs 1)

14. Don't talk behind someone's back and then give them a kiss. That's to be avoided and it's called _____. (1 wd, vs 3)

15. Be _____, be poised, be eager to do good, because it brings fun results, not just because you should. (1 wd, vs 1)

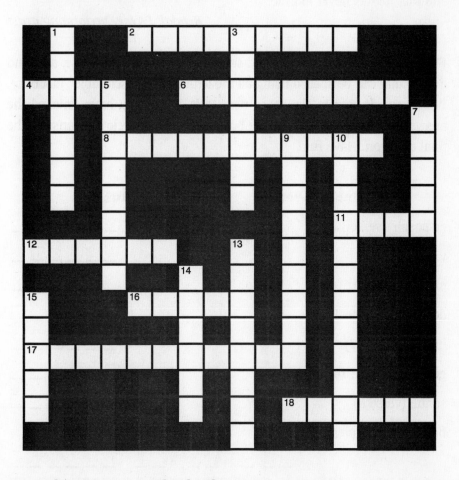

Something More to Think About: Read again Titus 3:5 and write in your journal what it means to you. Based on this verse, write out a prayer thanking God that you aren't a Christian because you act perfectly, but because you have received God's gift of grace.

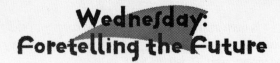

Wednesday: Foretelling the Future

Read Zechariah 9

Thought for Today: I'm all about hope. I am a Christian. I don't believe in beating people over the head with a Bible, but the only hope I have, the only reason I get up in the morning, is because I believe that God is there and that he has never left me.

Kendall Payne, performing artist

Puzzle: Today we have a word scramble! Look up each verse, and find a word that can be spelled using all the letters of the "scramble" just once. Write your answer in the space next to it. When you have finished the answer, transfer the letter in the box to the blanks below to answer the final question. Have fun!

Scrambled word	Solution
ersposnir (verse 12)	_ □ _ _ _ _ _ _ _
viesrl (verse 3)	_ _ _ _ □ _
pkeasrl (verse 16)	_ _ □ _ _ _ _
dcnesmuo (verse 4)	_ _ _ _ _ _ _ □
huotms (verse 7)	_ _ _ □ _ _
ginthnigl (verse 14)	_ _ _ □ _ _ _ _
sohue (verse 8)	_ _ _ _ □
biters fo eirsal (verse 1)	_ _ _ □ _ _ _ _ _ _ _ _ _
ignk (verse 9)	_ □ _ _
tieufbual (verse 17)	□ _ _ _ _ _ _ _
ipocmlrar cpaee (verse 10)	_ _ _ _ □ _ _ _ _ _ _ _ _

52

haneskol (verse 5)   _ _ _ _ _☐_ _ _

Transfer the boxed letters to find out how you can know the future.

_ _ _ _ / _ _ _ / _ _ _ _ _

Something More to Think About: What do you think teenagers these days have hope in? Ask several of your friends what they think about the future and write a short paragraph in your journal summarizing your findings. Also list what you have hope in—like going to heaven, knowing God has a plan for you, and so on. Then smile the rest of the day because you know God is in charge!

Thursday:
I'm Courageous and Strong

Read Joshua 1

Thought for Today: Courage and boldness come from caring about people more than you care about your own safety, security, and comfort. Don't be reckless, but don't play it too safe either.

Reggie White, professional football player

Joshua 1 Clues:

1. After the _____ of Moses the servant of the Lord (1 wd, vs 1)
2. The Lord said to Joshua _____ (3 wds, vs 1)
3. Now then, you and all these people, get _____ the Jordan River (3 wds, vs 2)
4. Into the land I am about to give to them—to the _____ (1 wd, vs 2)
5. Your _____ will extend from the desert to Lebanon (1 wd, vs 4)
6. From the great river, the _____—all the Hittite country—to the Great Sea (1 wd, vs 4)
7. I will be with you; I will _____ nor forsake you (3 wds, vs 5)
8. Be strong and _____, because you will lead these people (1 wd, vs 6)
9. _____ to obey all the law (2 wds, vs 7)
10. Do not turn from it to the right or to the left, that you may be _____ wherever you go (1 wd, vs 7)
11. _____ on it day and night (1 wd, vs 8)
12. _____, for the Lord your God will be with you wherever you go (4 wds, vs 9)
13. Three days from now you will _____ the Jordan (1 wd, vs 11)
14. But to the _____ (1 wd, vs 12)
15. Your _____ may stay in the land (1 wd, vs 14)
16. You may go back and _____ your own land (1 wd, vs 15)
17. Just as we _____ Moses, so we will obey you (2 wds, vs 17)
18. Whoever _____ against your word (1 wd, vs 18)

Joshua 1

```
F  R  A  R  E  A  D  Y  T  O  C  R  O  S  S  R  N  L  N
V  F  U  L  L  Y  O  B  E  Y  E  D  V  R  S  E  D  L  H
D  Y  W  V  C  Y  N  G  T  O  B  E  A  R  D  P  B  S  K
T  E  R  R  I  T  O  R  Y  M  S  A  I  X  X  W  L  J  P
J  R  S  P  S  I  T  D  P  W  G  M  C  I  A  W  E  H  C
I  J  E  B  H  L  B  E  C  A  R  E  F  U  L  V  B  F  S
A  Z  I  B  Q  F  E  Q  S  D  Y  H  D  Y  R  A  S  Q  S
P  E  M  I  E  G  D  A  Y  D  V  J  M  D  M  X  Q  U  Z
Y  Y  B  X  P  L  I  V  E  S  T  O  C  K  T  V  U  M  O
C  S  U  C  C  E  S  S  F  U  L  N  H  S  O  B  X  D  X
S  V  M  L  Z  C  C  T  R  D  Q  Q  Q  C  S  D  F  P  X
J  U  P  M  H  K  O  D  E  A  T  H  K  R  R  X  Z  P  D
U  U  D  E  H  X  U  U  R  E  K  H  D  J  O  F  R  Q
J  V  X  O  R  E  R  C  R  M  J  L  H  R  X  L  S  B  G
G  G  N  V  U  V  A  L  M  A  O  D  I  A  T  A  C  S  P
K  P  J  U  B  Q  G  R  I  Y  G  J  F  T  K  W  T  E  S
T  K  E  R  O  N  E  V  E  R  L  E  A  V  E  Y  O  U  P
E  K  R  L  V  C  D  F  J  A  Z  B  O  A  D  S  E  P  S
R  C  H  R  D  J  C  S  O  N  O  F  N  U  N  C  B  H  W
N  B  G  Q  Y  R  E  U  B  E  N  I  T  E  S  E  B  R  I
A  V  J  Q  Z  Z  J  X  P  R  R  K  D  F  F  U  L  A  D
I  P  I  P  A  E  Y  O  Z  Y  Z  H  C  H  D  J  L  T  P
C  G  D  B  W  A  J  W  O  O  M  E  D  I  T  A  T  E  S
X  U  I  I  I  N  G  X  K  C  V  J  A  Q  P  N  K  S  E
```

Something More to Think About: What bold attitudes do you admire in others? Are they using this boldness for or against God? Boldness doesn't bring too much good if it's not used in the way God wants. What actions of courage do you want to adopt into your own life?

Friday:
Don't Fret, a Messiah Is Coming

Read Micah 5

Thought for Today: God doesn't have a skin. He doesn't give us something tangible we can physically hold on to. But he does give us, through the Bible and through Jesus, some moorings. They're things that don't change—truths that we can grab on to and hold no matter how we're feeling.

Jay Kesler, writer

Puzzle: Today we have a word scramble! Look up each verse, and find a word that can be spelled using all the letters of the "scramble" just once. Write your answer in the space next to it. When you have finished the answer, transfer the letter in the box to the blanks below to answer the final question. Have fun!

Scrambled word	Solution
trcwfihcta (verse 12)	_ _ _ _ _ _ _ [_] _
sraiyas (verse 6)	_ _ _ _ [_] _ _
puroto (verse 14)	_ _ _ _ [_] _
salhrma (verse 1)	[_] _ _ _ _ _ _
tedsyro (verse 10)	_ _ _ [_] _ _ _
hehersdp (verse 4)	_ _ _ _ [_] _ _
erlru (verse 2)	_ _ _ [_] _
hribt (verse 3)	[_] _ _ _ _
whsesor (verse 7)	_ _ _ _ [_] _ _
goisirn (verse 2)	_ _ _ [_] _ _ _
rtuhpmi (verse 9)	_ _ [_] _ _ _ _

naisdve (verse 5) _ □ _ _ _ _ _

ouygn nilo (verse 8) _ _ _ _ _ _ _ _ □

eradvc gaisem (verse 13) _ _ _ _ _ _ □ _ _ _ _ _

gtrdsohnsol (verse 11) _ _ _ _ □ _ _ _ _ _

envnegaec (verse 15) _ _ _ □ _ _ _ _ _

Transfer the boxed letters to find out when God knew he would send Jesus as the Messiah.

_ _ _ _ / _ _ _ / _ _ _ _ _ _ _ _ _

Something More to Think About: Jesus is the Messiah who fulfills the prophecies found in the book of Micah and the other Old Testament books. If you have a friend who is Jewish, ask that person about his or her expectations of a Messiah. Don't try to preach or say that your friend is wrong, but just listen and pray for your friend to come to know Jesus as his or her Messiah.

Weekend Workout: Action Toward Your Future

The future may seem like a long way away, but each day is your future and is important. It's not too early to be thinking of your occupation and even your husband or wife. Which one of these things could you do this weekend? Be sure to pray for God's guidance.

- Make a list of the things you think you'd like to do for a profession. Beside each one write down a reason you think you'd like it.

- Talk to your parents about one of their friends' jobs to see if you can visit that friend's workplace for an hour one afternoon to see what it's like. Maybe someone from church or an organization you attend has a job that you think would be interesting. Give that person a call this weekend to see if you could visit.

- Get a group of your friends together and make a list of the qualities you'd each like in your future husband or wife. If this won't work, write out your own list in your journal.

Week Five:

Quiet Times:
Sitting in God's Presence

Monday:
Let's Just Praise the Lord

Read 1 Chronicles 16

Thought for Today: In my prayers I thank God for all the things he has given me, all of the blessings of my career. I pray before a game, I pray before I go to sleep, when I get up, and when I'm on a trip when the plane lands.

Dikembe Mutombo, professional basketball player

Puzzle: Today let's go on a word search! First, solve the verse clues below. Then see how many you can find in the puzzle, looking from top to bottom, left to right, and diagonally.

1 Chronicles 16 Clues:

1. They brought the _____ of God (1 wd, vs 1)
2. Set it inside the tent that David had _____ for it (1 wd, vs 1)
3. After David had finished sacrificing the burnt offerings and _____ offerings (1 wd, vs 2)
4. He gave a loaf of bread, a _____ and a cake of raisins (3 wds, vs 3)
5. He _____ some of the Levites to minister (1 wd, vs 4)
6. To _____ the Lord, the God of Israel (1 wd, vs 4)
7. They were to play the _____ (3 wds, vs 5)
8. The priests were to blow the _____ regularly (1 wd, vs 6)
9. Give _____ to the Lord, call on his name (1 wd, vs 8)
10. _____ to him, sing praise to him (1 wd, vs 9)
11. _____ in his holy name (1 wd, vs 10)
12. Remember the _____ he has done (1 wd, vs 12)
13. O _____ of Israel his servant (1 wd, vs 13)
14. The _____ he swore to Isaac (1 wd, vs 16)
15. I will give the _____ as the portion (3 wds, vs 18)
16. They wandered from _____ to _____ (same 1 word, vs 20)
17. Do not touch my _____ ones (1 wd, vs 22)
18. Proclaim his _____ day after day (1 wd, vs 23)
19. All the gods of the nations are _____ (1 wd, vs 26)
20. Ascribe to the Lord glory and _____ (1 wd, vs 28)
21. The _____ is firmly established (1 wd, vs 30)
22. Then the trees of the _____ will sing (1 wd, vs 33)

Something More to Think About: Praise and thanksgiving are different. In your journal, write out one praise of God. Focus on one of his qualities, such as his love, kindness, graciousness, or mercy. Then thank God by focusing on how he has provided for you—his actions. Each time you pray, praise him for who he is and then thank him for what he does.

```
M L Z R U D L B M G G U S S I E U A O
C M Y N K W J H T A L B G G X N X Z G
H X T R O X A J S T Q R M H T A X K A
U E F T E N B N H T N E X Z H F L P B
P K D N Q S X D G Y Z S H H A S V J Q
Z N I I X N A R H D T E R N N P C K H
R H U D K F P N U L G E F A K E J H D
M B W L T X P D D B C X A T S A F R T
U Q S E Q G O A T H O N S I N G U O U
D I Z I Q A I D T Z A E A O R V P Y I
G E Y Q U Z N C P C R R G N S S R X U
I Z S M P E T B F O P Z P T T L G E J
S N F C A K E O F D A T E S Q E K C N
G J E C E G D R F X T P W L P M X B M
C S T R E N G T H U M D M Y C W H Y S
O D A Y A Z D K N U I S B B T A M E B
P P H L E F O A R K T D Y P Y B Q W W
Z C U H V L D T N T E P I B Q I N Y I
R N X V U A Z P I T C H E D N C N E F
S N X U X T T R N U S S C Y O H Q V B
U W M Q U W W I F W J M B E B L U F L
M N U T D O O K O T S I Q P F S S D G
Z E G R Y N R L G N Q C Y R M G P U W
R O W L A D L O P Q Y M L R A O W Y G
J B H L O E D L E K P W H A H T F F T
F Y E B F R B E T K S F O N O L G T V
T G O C Y S Y R R X V Z H F U T L C T
P U A P O B M H W M T O E C S Y V Z F
U T D V P E N C H D R I Z B C C S F T
W I G W P J I B S D L L N A I N E S E
```

Tuesday:
The Power of Prayer

Read James 5

Thought for Today: As we keep the communication up, we extend that prayerful attitude even throughout the day and are able to pray continually. We keep the phone line to the Father open and are ready to call him at any time of the day and tell him whatever is on our hearts.

Autumn Alcott, 1998 Brio Girl

James 5 Clues:

Across

3. He prayed again and the heavens gave _____. (1 wd, vs 18)
6. When your life seems defective, remember that prayer is _____ and effective. (1 wd, vs 16)
8. Elijah prayed _____. (1 wd, vs 17)
9. On happy days, sing _____. (3 wds, vs 13)
14. As the farmer waits for the ___ crop, you must wait for the Lord; do not stop! (1 wd, vs 7)
15. Do not swear—not by _____ or earth; if your "yes" is not yes it has no worth. (1 wd, vs 12)

Down

1. Take the ___ who spoke in the name of the Lord as your guide in patience even under the sword. (1 wd, vs 10)
2. Sin less and _____. (1 wd, vs 16)
4. You shouldn't leave the sick to boil, but anoint their heads with _____. (1 wd, vs 14)
5. God will always be there to answer your _____. (1 wd, vs 15)
7. Elijah was a man like _____, so why all the fuss? (1 wd, vs 17)
10. When you repent, you won't be forgotten but you will be _____. (1 wd, vs 15)
11. Pray when you are _____ and God will heal you quick. (1 wd, vs 14)
12. When your sins are revealed, you shall be _____. (1 wd, vs 16)
13. _____ are God's helpers. (1 wd, vs 14)

[Puzzle created by James Clausen, 11]

Something More to Think About: There are many different ways to pray. You can write out your prayers, pray a verse right from the Bible, shoot off an "arrow" prayer at any time (like "Help!"), or sit quietly in real concentration. Circle the types of prayer that you've already done and underline one that you'd like to try today. Then get excited about talking to God, because he loves to hear your voice.

Wednesday:
Remembering God's Mercies

Read Deuteronomy 10

Thought for Today: A "solitude of the heart" can be maintained when our focus is on him and our activities are monitored by an awareness of his presence.

Carol Kent, author and speaker

Puzzle: Today we have a word scramble! Look up each verse, and find a word that can be spelled using all the letters of the "scramble" just once. Write your answer in the space next to it. When you have finished the answer, transfer the letter in the box to the blanks below to answer the final question. Have fun!

Scrambled word

Solution

huagodgd (verse 7) ☐ _ _ _ _ _ _

etn memadnmcnots (verse 4)

_ _ _ _☐_ _ _ _ _ _ _ _ _

sesspos (verse 11) _☐_ _ _ _ _

edruib (verse 6) _ _ _ _ _☐

tumnoina (verse 1) _ _ _ _ _ _ _☐

neaocntv (verse 8) _ _ _☐_ _ _ _

aicaac odow (verse 3) _ _ _ _ _ _ ☐_ _ _

rotfy adsy dan shigtn (verse 10)

_ _ _ _ _ _ _ _☐ _ _ _ _ _ _ _ _ _

64

Transfer the boxed letters to find out what God wants to communicate with you.

_ _ _ _ / _ _ _ _

Something More to Think About: Take a survey among your Christian friends about how they stay tuned in with God. Write out the answers and then share your findings with your friends. You will be a messenger of good news!

Thursday:
Running From God and Regretting It

Read Jonah 1

Thought for Today: The first thing we're tempted to do when we sin is run from God.... God is full of grace—he is love personified. He wants us to admit our wrong and say we're sorry so he can renew and forgive us.

Greg Long, performing artist

Puzzle: Today let's go on a word search! First, solve the verse clues below. Then see how many you can find in the puzzle, looking from top to bottom, left to right, and diagonally.

Jonah 1 Clues:

1. The word of the Lord came to _____ (1 wd, vs 1)
2. Go to the great city of _____ (1 wd, vs 2)
3. And _____ against it (1 wd, vs 2)
4. But Jonah _____ from the Lord (2 wds, vs 3)
5. He found a _____ bound for that port (1 wd, vs 3)
6. Then the Lord sent a _____ on the sea (2 wds, vs 4)
7. He lay down and fell into a _____ (2 wds, vs 5)
8. Get up and call on your _____ (1 wd, vs 6)
9. Let us _____ to find out who is responsible for this calamity (2 wds, vs 7)
10. Tell us, who is _____ for making all this trouble for us? (1 wd, vs 8)
11. I am a Hebrew and I _____, the God of heaven (3 wds, vs 9)
12. Pick me up and _____ into the sea (2 wds, vs 12)
13. The men did their best to _____ back to land (1 wd, vs 13)
14. Do not hold us accountable for killing an _____ man (1 wd, vs 14)
15. Then they took Jonah and threw him _____ (1 wd, vs 15)
16. But the Lord provided a great _____ to swallow Jonah (1 wd, vs 17)

Jonah 1

```
L  H  U  K  Q  O  T  T  H  R  O  W  M  E  H  L  C  Z  N
I  B  N  J  K  Z  N  E  C  A  A  H  G  V  G  U  H  R  H
F  C  S  R  G  R  E  A  T  W  I  N  D  I  J  A  H  O  Y
H  H  H  Q  K  C  I  F  R  O  Y  I  A  M  O  H  I  Y  U
L  G  I  Z  H  E  H  Y  A  R  V  N  T  W  N  N  C  X  R
U  Q  P  H  L  H  R  N  Z  S  U  E  R  M  A  A  N  N  G
N  K  Z  H  Y  O  B  E  H  H  D  V  R  T  H  Y  A  R  V
W  E  F  F  S  Y  E  Z  S  I  Y  A  Y  B  G  X  U  R  C
G  H  C  L  O  X  X  J  I  P  G  H  U  I  O  G  W  A  W
P  D  Y  H  I  O  Y  G  S  T  O  Y  W  S  D  A  X  A  Y
S  B  T  F  J  F  I  S  H  H  V  N  V  H  H  G  R  B  K
E  N  R  Y  X  A  A  N  I  E  U  X  S  A  R  B  E  D  V
L  V  S  T  O  W  G  I  N  L  B  I  C  I  Z  Q  T  A  H
X  F  N  U  C  U  W  J  P  O  E  Y  X  D  B  L  K  X  K
X  W  J  T  H  Y  U  H  H  R  C  C  A  S  T  L  O  T  S
G  W  H  L  K  S  W  U  P  D  E  E  P  S  L  E  E  P  N
C  A  F  S  N  H  W  V  R  C  Z  A  N  H  G  O  Y  Y  O
W  M  K  Q  F  Y  D  W  M  O  P  T  C  T  S  T  U  H  Z
C  W  K  W  O  R  S  X  F  A  E  V  L  H  J  N  R  G  M
```

Something More to Think About: When have you felt like Jonah? Why were you afraid of God? Describe the situation in your journal, and then write about how it turned out. How do you think God felt when you ran from him? And how do you think he felt when you turned back? Remember that the next time you're tempted to run from God.

Friday:
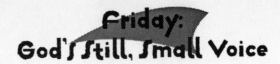
God's Still, Small Voice

Read 1 Kings 19

Thought for Today: I'm stunned—to think the Lord would enter into our lives and remain, like the perfect guest who you think is coming to visit but has decided, much to your delight, to stay. Not only will the Lord take up residence in our heart's home, but he will also lead and guide our decisions on which future doors we should enter. When opportunity knocks, it isn't necessarily in our best interest to step though every door. I'm grateful that the Lord offers to direct our steps.

Patsy Clairmont, writer and speaker

Puzzle: Today we have a word scramble! Look up each verse, and find a word that can be spelled using all the letters of the "scramble" just once. Write your answer in the space next to it. When you have finished the answer, transfer the letter in the box to the blanks below to answer the final question. Have fun!

Scrambled word	Solution
thersgentned (verse 8)	_ ☐ _ _ _ _ _ _ _ _ _
redstathe (verse 11)	_ ☐ _ _ _ _ _ _
travnse (verse 3)	_ ☐ _ _ _ _ _
baha (verse 1)	_ _ _ ☐
phirwse (verse 12)	_ _ ☐ _ _ _ _
keca fo debra (verse 6)	_ _ _ _ _ _ ☐ _ _ _ _
uazoels (verse 10)	_ _ _ ☐ _ _ _
nvoceatn (verse 14)	_ _ _ ☐ _ _ _ _

68

Transfer the circled letters to find out the sure way to know God's voice.

— — — / — — — — —

Something More to Think About: When you read about Elijah's encounter with God, how did you expect God to speak to Elijah? Were you surprised that he didn't use the earthquake, wind, or fire? After all, isn't that usually the way we think of his voice? How does God's voice within your mind or heart sound? If you haven't yet heard his voice, ask God to speak to you, but remember that the best way to hear God is through reading his words to us in the Bible.

Weekend Workout:
Spend Some Time With God

God wants to spend time with you! It doesn't have to be some mystical experience; just take some time to focus on him. Choose one of these ideas for growing closer to God.

If you're not in the habit of spending time daily with God, don't set a goal of doing it every day. It will be better to set a small goal, like, "I'm going to spend three minutes with God this weekend and two minutes next Tuesday and Thursday." Then, if you do more or do it more often, that's great, but don't think you have to spend an hour in order for it to be meaningful.

1. Get a group of friends together and read one chapter of the Bible. Talk about what it means to each of you.

2. Read one chapter of the book of Matthew and write down in your journal one thing you learned about Jesus.

3. Pray for three minutes, using this formula:

   • A: Adoration. Tell God one thing you appreciate about him, such as his love or patience for you.

   • C: Confession. Ask God to forgive you for any sins you can think of.

   • T: Thanksgiving. Thank God for how he's going to answer your prayers—even if it's in a different way than you were thinking about.

   • S: Supplication. Ask God for what you need, or ask him to meet the needs of someone else.

Week Six:

I'm a Child of:
the King

Monday:
I'm Connected to Jesus

Read John 15

Thought for Today: When I was seventeen, I came back to a disciplined relationship with him, and that ignited the fire within me to tell others about God. He's totally changed my life, and I want others to know that he can change their lives too!

Hanne Pettersen (Shine)

Puzzle: Today it's a crossword puzzle! Look up each verse listed below to find the word you need to fill in the clue either up and down or from left to right.

John 15 Clues:

Across

2. I am _____ by the Lord, tied into him strong—like a three-strand cord. (1 wd, vs 16)

4. I'm a _____ that bears much fruit; in God's garden I take root. (1 wd, vs 2)

6. As much as the Father _____ Jesus, Jesus _____ me. That's enough to set me free. (same 1 wd, vs 9)

9. God is the ____, we are the vines; he prunes us back to keep us in line. (1 wd, vs 1)

11. Want to know how to be Jesus' _____? Just do what he says and start a new trend. (1 wd, vs 14)

12. Jesus wants me to have full ____; and believe me, he's not being coy. (1 wd, vs 11)

14. _____ may sound awful, but it helps us to be more fruitful. (1 wd, vs 2)

Down

1. The Lord's _____ I must keep to remain in his flock, one of his sheep. (1 wd, vs 10)

3. With Jesus I can do anything, and without him I can do _____. (1 wd, vs 5)

5. When people see Jesus in me, that brings my Father _____. (1 wd, vs 8)

6. Our _____ for others should be true, and reflect the way that Jesus loves you! (1 wd, vs 12)

7. There's one and only one true _____, so don't let anyone give you a different line. (1 wd, vs 1)

8. I am not of this _____, it's not my home—no wonder my troubles can't make me moan. (1 wd, vs 19)

10. When in my heart Jesus reigns, I bear fruit and with him I'll _____. (1 wd, vs 4)

13. To remain in the Lord is the best thing you can do; then whatever you request "will be given ____." (1 wd, vs 7)

Something More to Think About: In your journal, draw a picture of a vine and then draw you clinging to the vine as one of the branches. Reread John 15 and then list the ways that Jesus flows into you: like through reading the Bible, asking for his help, and so on. Is your branch plump and green right now, or is it withered and malnourished? Either way, what does God want you to do to be nourished by him?

Tuesday:
I'm an Alien, You're an Alien Too

Read 1 Peter 2

Thought for Today: Always remember that maintaining a trustworthy reputation is one of the greatest assets in life—one developed through diligent, responsible action. To develop this characteristic, simply say what you are going to do, and do what you say consistently over time.

John Crudele, youth speaker

1 Peter 2 Clues:

1. Rid yourselves of all _____ (1 wd, vs 1)
2. Like _____, crave pure spiritual milk (2 wds, vs 2)
3. The _____—rejected by men but chosen by God (2 wds, vs 4)
4. Are being built into a spiritual house to be a _____ (2 wds, vs 5)
5. I lay a stone in Zion, a chosen and _____ cornerstone (1 wd, vs 6)
6. The stone the builders rejected has become the _____ (1 wd, vs 7)
7. A stone that causes men to _____ (1 wd, vs 8)
8. You are a chosen people, a _____ priesthood (1 wd, vs 9)
9. Once you had not received _____ but now you have received _____ (same 1 wd, vs 10)
10. As _____ and strangers in the world, to abstain from sinful desires (1 wd, vs 11)
11. Live such _____ among the pagans (2 wds, vs 12)
12. _____ yourselves for the Lord's sake to every authority (1 wd, vs 13)
13. By doing good you should silence the _____ of foolish men (2 wds, vs 15)
14. Live as _____ (3 wds, vs 16)
15. Love the brotherhood of believers, _____ God (1 wd, vs 17)
16. Slaves, submit yourselves to your masters with all _____ (1 wd, vs 18)
17. It is commendable if a man _____ under the pain of unjust suffering (2 wds, vs 19)
18. If you _____ and you endure it, this is commendable before God (4 wds, vs 20)
19. Christ suffered for you, leaving you an _____ (1 wd, vs 21)
20. He himself bore our _____ in his body on the tree (1 wd, vs 24)
21. For you were like _____ going astray (1 wd, vs 25)

74

```
G O T Q J R U Y Z G L V H N J X D I M
W I T S V R A N S C C J Y Z G J I K M
F B H E A H L I R D I I I Q E U I D Z
U Y N E W B O R N B A B I E S O O D L
E M F Q E B Q L I V I N G S T O N E C
I W X A N A T T Y W G K R C G G B Z X
B O C H U A T D U P M Q K G Z E U Z U
R E A R M K O C J U R A N S P K B Y Z
K R A L H Y F A J P E I I E C O W K X
L F M Y B G Q P U D O N E L E Z L P S
H I M F Y P Z S R D F H M S I A S I N
J S D B F S R T R E S P E C T G H R M
X H Z S X A I O K O S J E T G H S X M
V S W Y E M F N S M Y A N I N S O T U
E Q J B B R W E S K W A L Q C V S O S
C C K U E O V V E P R W L C L S Y U D
O X S F T I V A U O J E M R I S I C E
J N F A L Q O B N E E M A W A E J E D
Y U Z D G R S G M T V A G N Y Q L W Z
S V O K J S I F A O S P L G N P C J I
L O M J Z N H G W U T O A I M T R G C
G S G W N P D O E D V S F A E E T B P
G U M E T D I W Q N J T X G C N R W C
J C X J G I Z J I P R E C I O U S C C
Y R B X Y Z U C Y T S Q L A D D H T Y
L P W H I Z P L F C R A G E D J Y D E
M D S V T K H Y Y N M I G A Q H F Q M
J I F P Y L H O A O C J D T W C S Q S
L L N K X H Q Q A C D Q B P M Q A Z B
U H T S X G J E L B M U T S G C R F G
```

Something More to Think About: As a member of God's family, you are like an alien on earth—your citizenship is in heaven. That means you can live differently from the way some people live on earth, when they make wrong choices. What would you say your reputation is among others? Do you mind being considered "a Christian"? Is there something you need to do to shine up your reputation?

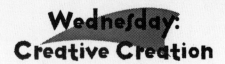

Wednesday:
Creative Creation

Read Genesis 1 and 2

Thought for Today: I am here for a purpose. God wouldn't have taken time to create me if he didn't have a purpose for me being here. And if he did create me, he must know me so well that he knows what I need even more than I know.

Ginny Owens, performing artist

Genesis 1–2 Clues:

Across

1. _____ covered the surface of the deep before there was anyone to sleep. (1 wd, 1:2)

3. _____ was the first man's name; in God's image was his earthly frame. (1 wd, 2:20)

5. In the waters and streams, _____ teemed. (1 wd, 1:20)

6. The _____ of Eden God formed in the East; here he placed Adam and the birds and the beasts. (1 wd, 2:8)

7. _____ created the heavens and the earth, a home for us of incomparable worth. (1 wd, 1:1)

9. God made a _____ out of a rib, then the serpent tricked her with a fib. (1 wd, 2:22)

11. The ___ was the day's end, when the sun would descend. (1 wd, 1:8)

14. The clay God didn't even bake, yet _____ in his own image did he make. (1 wd, 1:26)

15. What can you find that bears fruits after its kind? (1 wd, 1:12)

16. God created _____ on the second day; it made the darkness go away. (1 wd, 1:3)

18. God created these smaller lights, which we can only see at night. (1 wd, 1:14)

Down

2. God _____ on the seventh day and said, "Hey, this world is OK!" (1 wd, 2:2)

4. Evening and _____ made up the first day; night and day too in the natural way. (1 wd, 1:5)

7. What dry thing appeared when God separated the waters by his word? (1 wd, 1:9)

8. _____ was produced by God's hand on the land. (1 wd, 1:12)

10. God created the _____ on the sixth day, the wild and the mild, the predator and the prey. (1 wd, 1:25)

12. _____ was the earth before its birth. (1 wd, 1:2)

13. These God put an expanse between so his power could be seen. (1 wd, 1:6)

17. What did God say his creation was? (1 wd, 1:10)

[Puzzle created by Katie Knickerbocker]

Something More to Think About: When you look at all the things God created in our world, which part of creation seems the most entertaining to you? A long-necked giraffe or a round hippopotamus? How do you think God looks at each part of his creation? If you find yourself laughing at others because of the way they were created, just remember that each person is created by God!

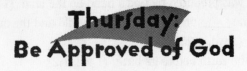

Thursday:
Be Approved of God

Read 2 Timothy 2

Thought for Today: Winners turn stress into something good; losers let stress turn life into something bad. Winners see an answer for every problem; losers see a problem for every answer.

Barbara Johnson, speaker and author

Puzzle: Today we have a word scramble! Look up each verse, and find a word that can be spelled using all the letters of the "scramble" just once. Write your answer in the space next to it. When you have finished the answer, transfer the letter in the box to the blanks below to answer the final question. Have fun!

Scrambled word   **Solution**

iegtchan (verse 17)   _ _ _ _ ☐ _ _ _ _

lafistehs (verse 13)   _ _ _ _ _ _ _☐ _ _

ngtlye ntrsictu (verse 25)   _ _ _ _☐ _   _ _ _ _ _ _ _ _

daoprvpe (verse 15)   _ _ _ _☐ _ _ _

tsnrvea (verse 24)   _ _ _☐ _ _ _

ungrqreial (verse 14)   _ _ _ _ _☐ _ _ _ _

edglsos tecahtr (verse 16)   _ _ _ _ _ _ _☐   _ _ _ _ _ _ _

houty (verse 22)   ☐ _ _ _ _

seorurtiernc (verse 18)   _ _ _ _ _ _ _ _ _ _☐ _

loebn ousrpeps (verse 20)   _ _ _ _ _ _   _☐ _ _ _ _ _ _

eivdl (verse 26)   _ _ _ _☐

loiosfh (verse 23)   _☐ _ _ _ _ _

78

datsns mirf (verse 19)   _ ☐ _ _ _ _   _ _ _ _

menusritnt (verse 21)   _ _ ☐ _ _ _ _ _ _ _

Transfer the boxed letters to find out why you can trust God's purposes for you.

_ _ / _ _ _ _ _ _ / _ _ _ / _ _ _ _

Something More to Think About: God has "noble purposes" for you. Can you think of someone who has been an example to you of waiting on God for his purposes for them? What were you impressed about in how they trusted God? How are you inspired to do the same?

Friday:
There's No Secret Too Small!

Read Psalm 139

Thought for Today: As Christians, we all need to step forward and show people that it's Christ's love in us that makes the difference. We're all God's creation, and we should love one another.

Bill Brooks, professional football player

Puzzle: Today it's a crossword puzzle! Look up each verse listed below to find the word you need to fill in the clue either up and down or from left to right.

Psalm 139 Clues:

Across

2. You are familiar with all my _____, in all I do, in all my days. (1 wd, vs 3)

3. Your love is as clear as the light of _____ at each new day. (1 wd, vs 9)

4. You _____ me together before my birth; you know all my ways upon the earth. (1 wd, vs 13)

6. You ____ me in, behind and before; you watch over my steps at each new door. (1 wd, vs 5)

7. Another word for find or seek. (1 wd, vs 1)

10. You are the _____ that helps me see. Because you are near, from harm I am free. (1 wd, vs 11)

12. I open this book of _____ to take an inside peek; your treasures are all I seek. (1 wd, vs 6)

13. Where can I go from your ___? No distance is too far from your voice to hear it. (1 wd, vs 7)

14. I can walk on the _____, even against the tide, as long as you are by my side. (1 wd, vs 9)

Down

1. If I make my ___ in the depths you are there; I cannot escape your loving care. (1 wd, vs 8)

2. Don't stop now, I'm not finished yet; your _____ I will never forget. (2 wds, vs 14)

5. Before I think, before I speak, you know what fills my mind, which are these. (1 wd, vs 2)
8. You hold this out, and I won't let go as I move about. (1 wd, vs 10)
9. From your presence no one can ____; from your spirit we are never free. (1 wd, vs 7)
11. In all my speech, and the songs I've sung, you know my words before they leave my _____. (1 wd, vs 4)

[Puzzle created by Nicole Howe and Katlyn Howe]

Something More to Think About: It's hard sometimes to remember that God had each of us in mind even when we were being formed as babies in our mothers' wombs. You were not a mistake, and God didn't make junk when he made you. Write down in your journal, "God didn't make junk when he made me. I was thought of by God from the very beginning." Then think about how special you are to God.

Weekend Workout: What's Your Spiritual Heritage?

Did you know that you're someone special—a child of the King Jesus? The Bible says that you are a part of the body of Christ and that you are important and valuable. Here are some ideas for making that more real. Choose one.

1. With a friend, make a crown to wear and really make it pretty, with glitter and paint. Write the word "Princess" or "Prince" on it. Wear it around the house for awhile to make your position in Christ more real to you. (You might not want to answer the door with it on, though!)

2. If you want another Scripture assignment this weekend, look at Ephesians 1 and list all the things it says you have because you're a Christian—things like "every spiritual blessing" and "forgiveness." See how many you can come up with. There are lots!

3. If you're not sure whether you are a Christian, or if you know you've never invited Jesus into your heart, say this prayer: "Heavenly Father, thank you for sending Jesus to die for me. I know I've done many things wrong and want to be forgiven. Please forgive me and come into my heart as my Lord and Savior. Thank you that you've done this because you love me so much." Regardless of how you feel, Jesus is in your heart. Write today's date in your Bible and beside it, write, "The day I became a Christian by asking Jesus into my heart."

Week Seven:

With God, All Things Are Possible

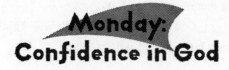

Monday:
Confidence in God

Read Lamentations 3

Thought for Today: I realize that going through the struggles was the best thing for me. What I learned from the tough times was that sometimes, what we think is best for us, isn't. All the talents I've been given are a direct reflection of God. Without him, I wouldn't have anything.

Kim Young, gymnast

Puzzle: Today it's a crossword puzzle! Look up each verse listed on the next page to find the word you need to fill in the clue either up and down or from left to right.

Lamentations 3 Clues:

Across

3. When God brings affliction, he's not cheering with glee. There's a purpose in it but he doesn't do it _____. (1 wd, vs 33)

4. Even when we goof we can sing this song, "his ____ never fail" and he won't treat us wrong. (1 wd, vs 22)

6. When life seems like the pits, just _____: there is a truth you already know—God is loving and kind. (3 wds, vs 21)

8. The Lord is my ____; therefore will I wait. The time spent will be worth it, for something so great. (1 wd, vs 24)

10. God's love is a _____, coming straight from heaven above. (2 wds, vs 22)

12. _____ far away from God only worsens our pain. If we run toward him, he will ease the strain. (1 wd, vs 19)

13. When a friend keeps loving you even when you make a mistake, that's _____—isn't it great? (1 wd, vs 23)

15. The one who _____ God wants to know God's will. Think about him often—that's not a bitter pill. (1 wd, vs 25)

Down

1. God's love is ____ through all our years. He will be there through our joys and our fears. (1 wd, vs 32)

2. Every ____ God's compassions are new; through each day's trials he will be true. (1 wd, vs 23)

5. God is always _____ to you, no matter what happens. That's because he filters all your life through his loving lens. (1 wd, vs 25)

7. To _____ in God is not the same as hoping you'll know the answers to a test. It's knowing God's love and leaving everything else to rest. (1 wd, vs 21)

9. Sometimes our disobedience makes us _____, but seeking God's forgiveness is all he asks. (1 wd, vs 20)

11. Though God brings ____ he always shows compassion; so keep him always in your heart, faith is never out of fashion. (1 wd, vs 32)

12. To ____ is not easy, even on the Lord, but for your patience there will be a reward. (1 wd, vs 24)

14. Though you may bury your ____ in the dust, there is always hope. God is always by your side, there to help you cope. (1 wd, vs 29)

Something More to Think About: Look back at a time when you experienced something very difficult. How did God bring something good out of it? Thinking about that will build your confidence in God—that he knows what he's doing even with the bad things in our lives.

Read Luke 2

Thought for Today: You may think it's pretty cool to pull off a hard trick or to see your face on ESPN, but it doesn't compare with knowing and following the Son of God—Jesus Christ.... He's the One who keeps me going and motivates me to ride well.

Tony Alvarez, stunt rider/flatland freestyle biking

Luke 2 Clues:

Across

5. The angel said "Do not be _____. I bring you good news of great joy." With that the shepherds' fear disappeared and they went to see the boy. (1 wd, vs 10)

6. Not knowing that his life was in danger, Mary placed the King of Kings in a _____. (1 wd, vs 7)

8. Caesar Augustus issued a ____: a census was to be taken of all people, slave and free. (1 wd, vs 1)

10. A _____ was to be taken of the entire Roman world; into the great migration Joseph and Mary were swirled. (1 wd, vs 1)

11. Shepherds living in the _____, suddenly saw angels appear in the sky. (2 wds, vs 8)

14. Mary _____ to a baby boy, and named him Jesus with great joy. (2 wds, vs 7)

15. This will be a sign, the heavenly angel said: you will find him _____ in cloths, with a manger for a bed. (1 wd, vs 12)

Down

1. The people were _____ at the story of Christ's birth; and so the message spread to the edges of the earth. (1 wd, vs 18)

2. The shepherds knew they must _____ the word. This great good news must be heard. (1 wd, vs 17)

3. The shepherds lost no time. "Let's _____," they chimed. (3 wds, vs 15)

4. A _____ host of angels appeared, praising God in the highest as the shepherds cheered. (1 wd, vs 13)

7. Mary, Jesus' mother, was in awe at what God had done. She _____ up all these things about her very own Son. (1 wd, vs 19)

9. Mary was _____ a child, when they for the census filed. (1 wd, vs 5)

12. He was born in a manger, for there was no room at the _____. What a humble beginning for the one who would conquer sin! (1 wd, vs 7)
13. To _____ Joseph and Mary headed as a pair, expecting that God would fulfill prophecy there. (1 wd, vs 4)
14. An angel with _____ had good news to tell, "Go see the baby who will vanquish hell." (1 wd, vs 9)

Something More to Think About: Why do you think it was necessary for Jesus to be born in a stable when he deserved to be in a palace? Now think about how you may be dissatisfied with your family or where you live. God has his own ideas about where he wants you—even if you have a brother or sister who bugs you or your parents can't afford the clothes you want. What is God building within you because of these kinds of things?

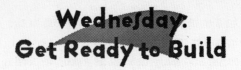

Wednesday:
Get Ready to Build

Read Ezra 3

Thought for Today: If I'd given in to the jungle of peer pressure, I would have been disappointed in myself no matter how much money or fame I'd come away with. Even if the in-group on the island—or the in-group anywhere—can't live with me, I have to live with myself.

Dirk Been, contestant on TV show "Survivor"

Puzzle: Today let's go on a word search! First, solve the verse clues below. Then see how many you can find in the puzzle, looking from top to bottom, left to right, and diagonally.

Ezra 3 Clues:

1. The _____ had settled in their towns (1 wd, vs 1)
2. His associates began to _____ of the God of Israel (3 wds, vs 2)
3. In accordance with what is written in the _____ (3 wds, vs 2)
4. Sacrificed _____ on it to the Lord (2 wds, vs 3)
5. They built the altar on its _____ (1 wd, vs 3)
6. They celebrated the _____ of Tabernacles (1 wd, vs 4)
7. On the first day of the _____ they began to offer burnt offerings (2 wds, vs 6)
8. They gave _____ to the masons and carpenters (1 wd, vs 7)
9. Gave food and drink and _____ to the people of Sidon and Tyre (1 wd, vs 7)
10. Appointing _____ twenty years of age and older (1 wd, vs 8)
11. To supervise the building of the _____ of the Lord (1 wd, vs 8)
12. The _____ in their vestments and with trumpets (1 wd, vs 10)
13. He is _____; his love to Israel endures forever (1 wd, vs 11)
14. _____ aloud when they saw the foundation of this temple being laid (1 wd, vs 12)
15. The people made so much _____ (1 wd, vs 13)

Ezra 3

```
E  E  L  Q  O  Y  C  J  X  X  L  Y  R  U  H  B  F
J  I  P  H  L  A  R  Z  F  Y  E  N  Y  F  K  R  O
U  K  S  O  Q  X  D  F  D  F  D  X  M  I  G  M  U
X  U  W  U  L  H  C  E  Y  N  D  X  J  D  O  D  N
X  H  F  S  F  B  Q  L  W  S  W  U  S  X  W  D  D
B  S  D  E  E  N  B  A  H  N  N  N  V  D  H  B  A
P  H  I  V  A  G  I  W  O  A  B  T  I  C  X  X  T
S  L  X  E  S  O  M  O  I  L  U  E  R  S  R  D  I
B  U  R  N  T  O  F  F  E  R  I  N  G  S  O  G  O
W  E  P  T  E  D  U  M  Y  S  L  A  M  W  G  T  N
Q  I  P  H  U  Z  P  O  R  O  D  M  F  J  P  I  S
I  Y  P  M  N  O  I  S  E  Q  T  P  P  O  R  S  S
H  H  M  O  N  E  Y  E  F  H  H  M  F  B  I  Q  Q
G  K  O  N  F  X  I  S  R  A  E  L  I  T  E  S  T
V  P  G  T  S  R  G  F  J  I  A  P  E  Q  S  V  X
M  D  Q  H  A  F  L  B  N  S  L  E  V  I  T  E  S
E  E  A  I  P  D  I  R  J  Y  T  C  G  F  S  P  M
C  X  U  S  B  Y  W  L  P  B  A  I  N  O  E  I  Q
Z  H  G  K  V  K  P  Q  S  Q  R  K  M  Q  F  Q  E
```

Something More to Think About: Ezra was a person who did what God wanted him to do, regardless of whether it was popular. Are you like that? Who is an example for you of that? What are you facing right now that makes you think you'd rather go with the crowd than with God's ideas? Pray about that right now.

Thursday:
Gettin' Ready to Visit a King

Read Nehemiah 1–2

Thought for Today: Our relationship with God is not a question of our ability to hang on to him. That really isn't within our personal power to do anyway. The fact is, God holds on to us, and he has the power to keep us securely and safely in his hand.

Neil T. Anderson, writer

Nehemiah 1–2 Clues:

Across

6. Though deeply saddened, Nehemiah knew what to do. He fasted and _____, do you do that too? (1 wd, 1:4)

9. Our Lord is a great and _____ God; those who love and obey him need not fear the rod. (1 wd, 1:5)

10. Confessing our _____ is an important part of prayer. Don't forget it, it clears the air. (1 wd, 1:6)

11. Timber from the _____ was to be used, to make replacement gates for those so recently abused. (2 wds, 2:8)

13. Nehemiah prayed for favor and _____, so that the king might grant his request. (1 wd, 1:11)

14. Do you want _____ for the things you need? Do what Nehemiah did, get on your knees. (1 wd, 2:5)

15. Hearing bad news can depress your mood. No wonder Nehemiah _____, prayed, and went without food. (1 wd, 1:4)

16. In his request Nehemiah did not waver. His plan to rebuild _____ with the king found favor. (1 wd, 2:5)

Down

1. It wasn't a coincidence that the king granted Nehemiah's requests. It was God's _____ hand and Nehemiah knew that's the best. (1 wd, 2:8)

2. For letters to the _____ Nehemiah asked, to guarantee his safety as he did his task. (1 wd, 2:7)

3. _____, Nehemiah shot up an arrow prayer. You too can do that any time because you know God does care. (3 wds, 2:2)

4. Nehemiah couldn't hide his _____; and so with the king's favor for Judah he did depart. (3 wds, 2:2)

5. A _____ has a very important job for the king. He tastes the wine to

make sure it's safe from poisoning. (1 wd, 1:11)

7. _____ lay in ruins; its gates had been burned. Yet Nehemiah knew that to good it could be turned. (1 wd, 2:13)

8. "How long will your journey take, and when will you get _____?" The king asked for a schedule to keep him on track. (1 wd, 2:6)

12. The gates of Jerusalem had been _____ with fire. To rebuild them was Nehemiah's desire. (1 wd, 1:3)

Something More to Think About: How would you have felt if you were Nehemiah, getting ready to go in to visit a king? (By the way, if the king was in a bad mood and didn't want to see you, he might have had you killed!) Did you notice Nehemiah's "arrow" prayer of "Help!"? The next time you feel scared about having to go talk to someone, like a teacher or a coach or even your parents, say a quick arrow prayer of "Help, Lord!" and see how God answers. Write about it in your journal if you can remember something like this happening to you in the past.

Listen to Gideon's Call

Read Judges 6

Thought for Today: Some degree of fear is healthy, because people who don't have any fear usually end up dying. But you can't let fear control you. My faith in God doesn't get rid of my fear, but it does help me deal with it. And some days are better than others.

Katie Brown, rock climbing champion

Puzzle: Today it's a crossword puzzle! Look up each verse listed below to find the word you need to fill in the clue either up and down or from left to right.

Judges 6 Clues:

Across

2. In a winepress Gideon was _____, to prevent it from becoming a Midianite treat. (2 wds, vs 11)

5. The angel told Gideon "the _____," and though hard to believe, he found it was true. (4 wds, vs 12)

6. "_____," the Lord said, we will strike the Midianites dead. (5 wds, vs 16)

9. The people had heard of God's _____ from the past, and wanted God to do the same—and fast! (1 wd, vs 13)

11. _____ from the rock, consuming meat and bread, and he recognized the angel, filling him with dread. (2 wds, vs 21)

12. "Go in the ____ you have," said the Lord, and save Israel from the Midianite hordes. (1 wd, vs 14)

13. Gideon set out a ____ on the floor; though God had already proven himself, Gideon asked for more. (1 wd, vs 37)

14. "_____" was Gideon's God-given name, yet he feared he could not live up to the claim. (2 wds, vs 12)

Down

1. Gideon wanted to believe God's words of _____, so he asked for a sign, that his faith might not waver. (1 wd, vs 17)

3. When he recognized the angel, Gideon gave a fearful cry, but the Lord said

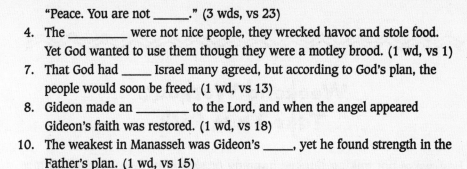

"Peace. You are not _____." (3 wds, vs 23)

4. The _____ were not nice people, they wrecked havoc and stole food. Yet God wanted to use them though they were a motley brood. (1 wd, vs 1)

7. That God had _____ Israel many agreed, but according to God's plan, the people would soon be freed. (1 wd, vs 13)

8. Gideon made an _____ to the Lord, and when the angel appeared Gideon's faith was restored. (1 wd, vs 18)

10. The weakest in Manasseh was Gideon's _____, yet he found strength in the Father's plan. (1 wd, vs 15)

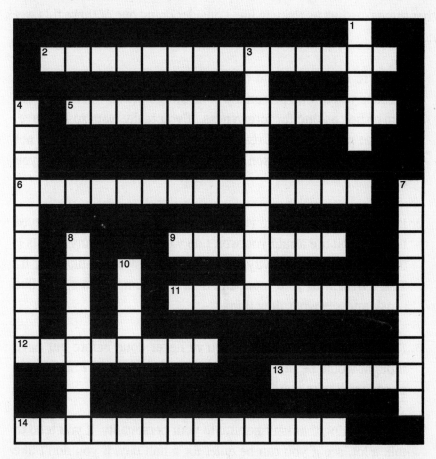

Something More to Think About: Gideon may not have considered himself a great man, but he sure was persistent in trying to convince God he wasn't. Do you do that? Do you argue with God about some of the risky things he wants you to do? The next time you find yourself arguing with God, just imagine him standing patiently, waiting for you to see that he's right. And remember the great victories Gideon had when he obeyed God.

Weekend Workout: Take That Risk

Hey, we're not talking bungee jumping or skydiving here! Yet sometimes other things are just as risky in life. Consider doing one of these this weekend.

1. If you're mad at a friend or are no longer friends with someone because you or that person did something hurtful, write a letter to him or her, asking for forgiveness. If you really want to be brave, call that person up and read the letter to him or her. Be sure not to blame the other person; just take responsibility for what you did.

2. If there's something you've been wanting to do but have delayed because you are afraid you won't do well at it, do it anyway! Is it a sport or another activity that makes you sweat thinking of it? Talk it over with your mom and dad. Tell them why it seems like a risk and see what they think.

3. Do something this weekend you've never done before but have thought would be fun. Is there a ropes course nearby? See if your parents will take you.

4. Do something that isn't natural to your personality. If you tend to talk a lot, see if you can be quiet for a half day. If you don't like to read, take time to read one chapter from a book. Do whatever is the opposite of your normal activity or preferences.

Week Eight:

This Fruit Isn't to Eat!

Monday:
Walking in the Spirit

Read Galatians 5

Thought for Today: No matter how much we'd like to be perfect, we're still going to make mistakes. But the best thing about mistakes is what we can learn from them. Not only can we learn from our own mistakes, but we can learn from the mistakes other people make, too.

Martha Bolton, writer for teens

Puzzle: Today it's a crossword puzzle! Look up each verse listed on the next page to find the word you need to fill in the clue either up and down or from left to right.

Galatians 5 Clues:

Across

1. You will be defeated if you are _____. (1 wd, vs 26)

2. _____ gracious, look at that mess. Just pick it up and you'll be blessed. (1 wd, vs 22)

4. In tennis, _____ means nothing, but in real life, it's everything. (1 wd, vs 13)

6. Even if someone gives you a miscue, I know you won't take any other _____. (1 wd, vs 10)

7. When you show this, then you'll know you are showing self-control. (1 wd, vs 22)

9. If you want to look at _____, head to the Yellowstone wilderness. (1 wd, vs 22)

10. Your hair and eyes can come from your parents, but God gives you a greater _____. (1 wd, vs 21)

12. Teasing others may seem like fun, but _____ out, one day you might be the one. (1 wd, vs 15)

Down

1. Which one are you going to pick? The Spirit and the sinful nature are in _____. (1 wd, vs 17)

3. Don't get out of _____. March in tune to the Spirit. (1 wd, vs 25)

4. Check out the list and don't _____ this. (2 wds, vs 21)

5. _____ are three fruits of the Spirit; follow God's ways and you'll come near it. (3 wds, vs 22)

7. Dress up your heart in godly fashions and you'll avoid sinful _____. (1 wd, vs 24)

8. Follow the _____ in your youth. (1 wd, vs 7)

9. It's never cute to neglect God's _____. (1 wd, vs 22)

11. Keep up the pace to win the _____. (1 wd, vs 7)

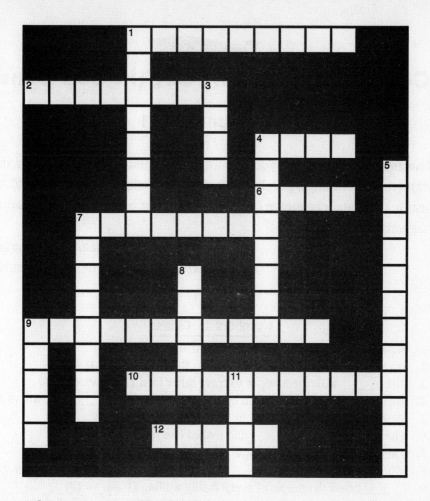

Something More to Think About: Walking in the power of the Holy Spirit doesn't make us perfect! That's not so bad, really—otherwise we might be tempted to look down at everybody else. If we were perfect, we wouldn't need to depend upon God. Is there an area in your life where your "imperfection" gives you an opportunity to trust God more?

Tuesday:
Complaining Doesn't Get the Job Done

Read Numbers 11

Thought for Today: If you're always complaining and looking for the negative side of things, people won't want your attitude. Strive, instead, to wear a smile and encourage others. This kind of positive attitude is what magnetizes people to you.

Susie Shellenberger
author of Help! My Friend's in Trouble

Numbers 11 Clues:

1. Now the people _____ about their hardships (1 wd, vs 1)
2. Because fire from the Lord had _____ them (2 wds, vs 3)
3. The _____ with them began to crave other food (1 wd, vs 4)
4. We remember the fish we ate in Egypt at no cost—also the _____ (1 wd, vs 5)
5. We never see anything but this _____ (1 wd, vs 6)
6. The manna was like _____ and looked like resin (2 wds, vs 7)
7. They cooked it in a pot or made it into _____ (1 wd, vs 8)
8. When the dew settled on the _____, the manna also came down (3 wds, vs 9)
9. _____ heard the people of every family wailing (1 wd, vs 10)
10. What have I done to displease you that you put the _____ of all these people on me? (1 wd, vs 11)
11. Why do you tell me to carry them in my arms, as a _____ an infant? (2 wds, vs 12)
12. They keep wailing to me, _____ to eat (3 wds, vs 13)
13. The burden is _____ for me (2 wds, vs 14)
14. Bring me _____ of Israel's elders (1 wd, vs 16)
15. I will come down and _____ there (3 wds, vs 17)
16. _____ yourselves in preparation for tomorrow (1 wd, vs 18)
17. But for a _____ (2 wds, vs 20)
18. Had them stand around _____ (2 wds, vs 24)
19. When the Spirit rested on them, they _____ (1 wd, vs 25)
20. _____ are prophesying in the camp (3 wds, vs 27)
21. _____ son of Nun, who had been Moses' aide (1 wd, vs 28)
22. Are you _____? (4 wds, vs 29)
23. While the meat was still between their _____ (1 wd, vs 33)

Numbers 11

```
J  E  J  M  K  C  I  J  F  P  X  W  T  X  O  Y  K  A  Q
K  I  N  E  I  H  X  L  O  A  L  A  K  G  E  K  D  U  G
I  S  U  B  A  T  C  O  N  S  E  C  R  A  T  E  G  A  Y
Q  Q  P  T  H  L  M  A  N  M  H  D  J  H  N  L  T  T  D
J  O  N  U  I  N  O  L  S  N  E  U  N  I  T  D  V  K  M
N  R  O  D  L  F  S  U  B  I  U  M  A  N  N  A  A  Z  I
B  J  Q  B  M  P  E  B  S  T  T  L  W  X  T  D  Y  L  M
J  A  J  D  C  V  S  E  S  F  P  L  O  J  E  A  G  U  I
M  K  J  D  I  Y  H  Z  N  M  O  S  E  V  E  N  T  Y  Z
F  A  L  G  R  P  Z  Y  O  L  Z  R  Y  W  O  D  B  D  C
C  J  S  E  O  Q  C  C  E  X  V  S  M  M  G  M  E  N  H
U  Q  M  R  J  I  W  H  W  X  X  P  A  Y  Q  E  E  W  I
P  I  P  F  J  Y  Q  X  H  X  I  D  L  U  S  D  M  H  E
F  Z  A  R  L  O  E  O  Q  J  E  M  O  R  R  A  C  O  E
R  M  L  R  I  V  A  L  S  N  H  Y  E  U  O  D  K  L  T
Z  Y  A  W  Q  D  N  R  R  E  H  D  B  W  D  U  B  E  X
E  R  C  H  D  N  E  U  Y  T  N  S  U  V  E  B  C  M  F
Y  Z  E  L  S  B  B  L  I  A  O  I  Q  C  A  R  C  O  F
D  Y  G  O  M  K  C  W  I  G  L  O  Z  R  K  H  S  N  M
H  G  I  U  S  O  K  R  D  F  F  T  H  E  T  E  N  T  T
Q  K  C  T  P  A  O  S  Y  Z  L  T  K  E  K  O  W  H  P
N  U  R  S  E  C  A  R  R  I  E  S  E  A  A  F  L  X  L
C  A  M  P  A  T  N  I  G  H  T  T  C  M  Q  V  V  B  L
O  R  S  N  X  M  W  F  X  G  Y  O  I  N  C  D  Y  M  B
```

Something More to Think About: Sometimes we complain and it just seems natural or needed at the moment. Yet we may not realize how we sound or how often we're doing it. Ask a friend and a member of your family, "Do I complain very much?" Be prepared for an answer you might not expect. If it comes, ask God to help you to be more positive and to see the sunny side of life.

Wednesday:
The Way to Peace and Joy

Read Philippians 4

Thought for Today: I'm aware that snowboarders are known for their drugs, alcohol, partying, and their casual sex ... kind of a free-spirited group. But I have chosen the different lifestyle that matches up with my faith, and while I don't go down the same run as many other snowboarders, I can still have fun.

Natalie Nelson, champion snowboarder

Philippians 4 Clues:

Across

1. When I admire someone, I say they are _____. (1 wd, vs 8)
4. That which is _____ is the truth—take the clue! (1 wd, vs 8)
8. Paul set himself up as a model to see, to _____ what he does is the key. (1 wd, vs 9)
9. Let your _____ be evident to all. The Lord is near; heed his call. (1 wd, vs 5)
12. God will help me do the _____ thing, when I let him be my heart's King. (1 wd, vs 8)
14. Things that are _____ are last on the list, but they are important and shouldn't be missed. (1 wd, vs 8)
15. Worry makes my heart feel sad, but _____ makes it feel real glad. (1 wd, vs 6)
16. God's peace will stand _____ at my heart, and then I'll sing with joy like a lark. (1 wd, vs 7)

Down

2. Paul said it once, and then again, "_____," savior of all men. (4 wds, vs 4)
3. God tells me not to _____ for anything, because he has his hand upon everything. (2 wd, vs 6)
4. Present your requests to God with _____ and he will take care of the life you are living. (1 wd, vs 6)
5. What's _____ or praiseworthy—think about such things; and see the joy God's presence brings. (1 wd, vs 8)
6. If we focus upon _____, we will avoid Satan's immoral lure. (3 wds, vs 8)
7. Whatever is true, _____, and right; think on these things as children of the light. (1 wd, vs 8)

10. Dwelling on _____ is another way to say, keep your mind on "goodness" replay. (2 wds, vs 8)
11. That which is _____ is a beautiful thought. Like blessing others with the positive—and doing it a lot. (1 wd, vs 8)
13. God has lots of good things for us in life. _____ on them and diminish strife. (1 wd, vs 8)

ſomething More to Think About: What is real joy? Some people think it's doing wrong things. What do you think? When are you most happy?

God says there's a difference between happiness and joy. Happiness is based on good things happening, but joy can come anytime as long as we trust God. Can you think of an unhappy time in your life when you trusted God to get you through it? That's joy. Write about it in your journal and repeat the story to a friend.

Thursday:
Living in the Hot Spots of Life

Read Daniel 3

Thought for Today: Any guy who wants you to compromise your personal, lifelong, biblical standards isn't worth having around anyway. When the pressure starts, eliminate the source of the irritation. Get rid of the influence.

Tom Tufts, youth speaker

Puzzle: Today we have a word scramble! Look up each verse, and find a word that can be spelled using all the letters of the "scramble" just once. Write your answer in the space next to it. When you have finished the answer, transfer the letter in the box to the blanks below to answer the final question. Have fun!

Scrambled word	Solution
galbizn ruacnfe (verse 6)	_ _ _ _ ☐ _ _ _ _ _ _ _ _ _
aeinctidod (verse 2)	_ _ _ _ _ _ ☐ _ _ _
elsdorsi (verse 20)	_ _ _ _ ☐ _ _ _
drsutte (verse 28)	_ _ _ ☐ _ _ _
nobeaedg (verse 12)	_ ☐ _ _ _ _ _
gikn dencabhanezuzr (verse 1)	_ _ _ _ _ _ _ _ _ _ _ ☐ _ _ _ _ _ _
cdrschoe (verse 27)	_ _ _ _ _ _ _ ☐
sliep fo brbleu (verse 29)	_ _ _ _ _ _ ☐ _ _ _ _ _ _ _
gimea fo odgl (verse 7)	_ _ _ _ _ _ _ _ ☐ _ _
gterosolasr (verse 8)	_ _ _ _ _ _ _ _ ☐ _
mzanaetme (verse 24)	_ ☐ _ _ _ _ _ _

ecreus (verse 15)   _ _ _ _ _ ☐

Transfer the boxed letters to find out why God wants you to resist temptation.

_ _ / _ _ / _ _ _ / _ _ _ / _ _

Something More to Think About: Shadrach, Meshach, and Abednego were amazing people, but God wants you to be just like them! He wants you to stand up for Jesus—no matter what happens. Is anyone pressuring you right now to do something you know is wrong? Tell someone—your parents, a Christian friend, or a church youth worker. These people will help you see how to resist that bad influence.

Friday:
Be Careful How You Drive

Read 2 Samuel 6

Thought for Today: I know I need to watch myself, because I don't want anyone to think I'm snobby or stuck-up. I have to be real careful. I don't want to hurt my Christian witness.

Austin O'Brien, actor

Puzzle: Today let's go on a word search! First, solve the verse clues below. Then see how many you can find in the puzzle, looking from top to bottom, left to right, and diagonally.

2 Samuel 6 Clues:

1. _____ again brought together out of Israel chosen men (1 wd, vs 1)
2. Men set out from Baalah of Judah to bring up from there the _____ (3 wds, vs 2)
3. They set the ark of God on a new cart and brought it from the _____ (3 wds, vs 3)
4. Ahio was _____ in front of it (1 wd, vs 4)
5. When they came to the _____ of Nacon (2 wds, vs 6)
6. The Lord's _____ against Uzzah (2 wds, vs 7)
7. Then David was angry because the Lord's _____ had broken out (1 wd, vs 8)
8. David was _____ of the Lord that day (1 wd, vs 9)
9. He was not willing to take the ark of the Lord to be with him in the _____ (3 wds, vs 10)
10. The Lord blessed him and his entire _____ (1 wd, vs 11)
11. The Lord has _____ the household of Obed-Edom (1 wd, vs 12)
12. He _____ a bull and a fattened calf (1 wd, vs 13)
13. David, wearing a _____, danced before the Lord (2 wds, vs 14)
14. Israel brought up the ark of the Lord with shouts and the sound of _____ (1 wd, vs 15)
15. As the ark of the Lord was entering the City of David, _____ daughter of Saul watched (1 wd, vs 16)
16. They brought the ark of the Lord and set it in its place inside the _____ (1 wd, vs 17)
17. After he had finished sacrificing the _____ (2 wds, vs 18)
18. Then he gave a _____ (3 wds, vs 19)

```
F X C E C H Q A V X M G A R N K H T S
R M M Q U V H D W U A P F O A X S N A
T T R U M P E T S H K W R I E G G U
Y U H B O E F V C I F R A L U F T T Y
W T B R M P A S Z U Y B I V W F A V E
H O U S E O F A B I N A D A B L D Q A
K A R N B S A C Y Z G T W R A T H U N
O F N W I U H R B G I P B K V W G B S
D H T E N T O I F I G U W O H J P G C
I Q O I K F L F N P D M L F U K X D U
L F F W A L K I N G M H O G M G P H T
B Y F M V B N C J U F T A O P R Q V U
N B E Z I H B E P O A L F D W D N K X
H S R I T C A D C I T Y O F D A V I D
J Q I W D T H A G G O L F O P Q N D J
W Y N R V L K A N G E R B U R N E D N
X W G C E I Z B L X N K R L T N K P R
D N S E S R D L I N E N E P H O D V U
R A H Y X L G E U X U S A P S X W B H
T M B Y H O U S E H O L D A K T M Z S
W W I I G N D S X N I W H R D M K X M
H O B H M B H E P N C G W A N O M X W
D A V I D W A D H O L L N T H Z C U H
```

Something More to Think About: Do you realize that you are being watched all the time, to see how you act as a Christian? You are. Draw a big set of eyes inside your school notebook to help you remember that eyes are watching you! Be the best you can be, to represent Jesus in the best possible way.

Weekend Workout:
Stop Worrying! It's a Dead-End Street!

Someone once said that worry is like a rocking chair: It gives you something to do but you don't go anywhere! How true! When we're worrying we're not accomplishing anything and we're being controlled by fear. Pick one of these worry-busters for this weekend.

- Put a rubber band on your wrist. Every time you start to worry about something, snap yourself! If you want to get your family into the act, convince them to put on rubber bands, too, and if you hear someone worrying, you can snap his or her rubber band!

- Get a 3 X 5 card and write the word "STOP" on one side in big letters. Then, on the other side, write out Philippians 4:6-7. Every time you realize you're starting to worry, pull out your card, say "STOP!" out loud twice, and turn the card over to read how you can stop that habit: through prayer and thanksgiving.

- When you start to worry, think of the worst possible thing that could happen and think of reasons why it wouldn't be so bad after all. Look up Romans 8:28 and see why you can think that way.

Worry is a habit. You will have to take steps like these for some time, but you can bust the worry habit!

Week Nine:

I'm Changing and Growing—
Inside, Too!

Monday:
Get Wise and Get Smart

Read Proverbs 1

Thought for Today: We want to challenge ourselves by reading. We like to read deep theological books and the classics, like *Moby Dick* and *The Brothers Karamazov*. We're thinking about all of us reading the same book and then discussing it. But we haven't agreed on one yet.

Luis Garcia (Plankeye)

Puzzle: Today it's a crossword puzzle! Look up each verse listed below to find the word you need to fill in the clue either up and down or from left to right.

Proverbs 1 Clues:

Across

2. No one really wants to be counted in with _____. Don't go there, it just isn't cool. (1 wd, vs 7)

3. _____ of the Lord doesn't mean cowering and being afraid, but coming in awe and recognizing God's helpful aid. (2 wds, vs 7)

5. There's always someone who has a plan to _____ you, but think quickly, "Will this to God keep me true?" (1 wd, vs 10)

6. Be careful who you pick for friends who promise _____ things. Make sure they're actually offering real winnings. (1 wd, vs 13)

8. Like a graceful garland on your ____ are your parents' instructions; by them be led. (1 wd, vs 9)

9. At times when the wise speak, it sounds like _____. But listen long enough and you'll learn lots—not just a little. (1 wd, vs 6)

11. It sure is good when we have someone share their _____, especially if we want to live well in God's kingdom. (1 wd, vs 2)

14. _____ may be an old-fashioned sounding word, but it basically means not doing something absurd. (1 wd, vs 4)

15. The feet of sinners _____. Don't follow along; they despise discipline. (3 wds, vs 16)

Down

1. Although not highly valued these days, _____ always pays. (4 wds, vs 3)

4. Your _____ may seem a bit odd, but listening always pleases God. (2 wds, vs 8)

7. There's always something we can _____ to our learning. So don't be foolish and think you know everything. (1 wd, vs 5)

10. The most important thing anyone can do is _____. If you do, you'll be considered a "10." (1 wd, vs 5)

12. Your _____ teaching may bug you some, but it's just because she loves you that she rattles your eardrum. (1 wd, vs 8)

13. _____ was the wisest man and he shared his proverbs—words of insight for living life in the city or the "burbs." (1 wd, vs 1)

Something More to Think About: Being smart has nothing to do with being wise. Being wise is seeing life through God's eyes. In what ways would you like to be wiser? Maybe in how you act toward a friend? Or maybe in getting along better with your parents? Ask God to help you and then memorize one of the verses from your reading today in Proverbs 1.

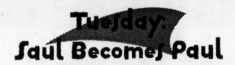

Saul Becomes Paul

Read Acts 9

Thought for Today: When we worship in spirit and truth, a change always occurs, as our attention lifts off ourselves and onto the beauty and majesty of God.

Martin Smith (Delirious)

Acts 9 Clues:

Across

1. _____ heard God's call and obeyed, though to help Saul he was afraid. (1 wd, vs 10)

5. The voice replied, "I am _____." Wasn't that the dead guy who started all this fuss? (1 wd, vs 5)

7. Can you imagine not seeing for _____? Saul must have felt like he was in a maze. (2 wds, vs 9)

8. A _____ asked "Why do you persecute me?" but who it was he couldn't see. (1 wd, vs 4)

9. Blind, Saul had to be led by _____. Once powerful, now he was not so grand. (2 wds, vs 8)

10. "Go into the _____," Saul heard Jesus say, and this he did right away. (1 wd, vs 6)

13. A bright _____ made him bow his knee to Jesus whom he didn't even see. (1 wd, vs 3)

14. The _____ fell from Saul's eyes; never again would he believe Satan's lies. (1 wd, vs 18)

15. First things first, before he ate, Saul was _____, and then loaded his plate. (1 wd, vs 18)

17. Taking _____ to Jerusalem was his goal and putting a spy in their camp—like "The Mole." (1 wd, vs 2)

18. The men with Saul looked around. No one was there, only the _____. (1 wd, vs 7)

Down

1. Ananias heard God call and he didn't like the message: "_____ for Saul." (1 wd, vs 11)

2. Ananias didn't want to be under _____. For helping Saul he didn't expect to be blessed. (1 wd, vs 14)

3. Saul was _____ out murderous threats; Christians always made him fret. (1 wd, vs 1)

4. To be God's _____ instrument was Saul's fate; in God's service his suffering would be great. (1 wd, vs 15)
6. Ananias' touch would _____ Saul's sight. He would help him see the truth and light. (1 wd, vs 12)
11. Saul just couldn't understand _____. For him to get to heaven a price he must pay. (2 wds, vs 2)
12. As Saul approached _____ he was surrounded by a light. The Lord was calling him; he could not fight. (1 wd, vs 3)
13. Wanting more power, Saul asked for _____ to allow him to put Christians into fetters. (1 wd, vs 2)
16. The light was so bright Saul had closed his eyes, but when he opened them again he was _____. Surprise! (1 wd, vs 9)

Something More to Think About: That was a dramatic way that Saul changed into Paul. Make a habit of asking other Christians how they came to believe in Jesus. You'll hear some interesting stories. Ask one Christian today about it and start the habit.

Wednesday:
Don't Mess With God

Read Nahum 1

Thought for Today: You may have never been in a gang. However, your problem may be pornography. It may be racism. It may be lying. It may be self-righteousness. God wants to break you down, he wants to strip you of whatever sin you have, and he wants to dress you up in the clothes of his righteousness.

Mr. Solo (Gospel Gangstaz)

Puzzle: Today let's go on a word search! First, solve the verse clues below. Then see how many you can find in the puzzle, looking from top to bottom, left to right, and diagonally.

Nahum 1 Clues:

1. An oracle concerning _____ (1 wd, vs 1)

2. _____ is a jealous and avenging God (2 wds, vs 2)

3. The Lord is _____ and great in power (3 wds, vs 3)

4. He _____ the sea and dries it up (1 wd, vs 4)

5. The _____ are shattered before him (1 wd, vs 6)

6. _____, a refuge in times of trouble (4 wds, vs 7)

7. He will pursue his _____ into darkness (1 wd, vs 8)

8. Whatever they _____ against the Lord he will bring to an end (1 wd, vs 9)

9. Now I will break their _____ from your neck (1 wd, vs 13)

10. Look, there on the mountains, the _____ of one who brings good news

    (1 wd, vs 15)

Nahum 1

```
        C S A            H T Q
      F Q S W W        B E H R I
    G Y P L O T        F E E T F K
  T I N U O J H W    V Z X L C V S N
  R O I P W U Y H S N M Y O K E B B
  E R N T T G F D S A R Z R X C V Y
  T H E L O R D I S G O O D P L M H
    S V E A W Q A S Y C U I O N U
      A Z N X C V F B K U J H P
      H A G S E R O Q S Q G Y O
        R E B U K E S I O J P
        R A W E S T P H J
          V S F C X
            C N C
              X
```

Something More to Think About: If you're a Christian, your spirit is clothed in Jesus' robe of righteousness. Right now, picture yourself wrapped in that luxurious robe. What does it feel like? What color is it? Does it have a hood? Is it fur-lined? Describe it in your journal and then thank God for giving you his righteousness, even though you can't earn it on your own.

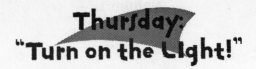

Thursday: "Turn on the Light!"

Read Ephesians 5

Thought for Today: Jesus does not call upon us to commit intellectual suicide in trusting him as Savior and Lord. He does not expect us to exercise our Christian faith in an intellectual vacuum. The Christian's faith must be based on the evidence.

Josh McDowell, youth writer and speaker

Puzzle: Today it's a crossword puzzle! Look up each verse listed below to find the word you need to fill in the clue either up and down or from left to right.

Ephesians 5 Clues:

Across

2. Live as children of _____; always do what's right. (1 wd, vs 8)

5. _____ is like a dove and comes from above. (1 wd, vs 2)

6. Let the _____ of the root bring forth righteousness, goodness, and truth. (1 wd, vs 9)

8. Do not be dumb and get _____ on rum. (1 wd, vs 18)

10. Since as God's holy people we have been freed, we should never show a hint of _____. (1 wd, vs 3)

13. Evil deeds we must _____, so that through us the Holy Spirit flows. (1 wd, vs 11)

15. Giving thanks means living a life of _____; that's how we live a life worth living. (1 wd, vs 20)

Down

1. Don't be in suspense or bored. Find out what pleases _____. (2 wds, vs 10)

3. Be _____ of God, Paul said; live a life of love and be Spirit-led. (1 wd, vs 1)

4. People who are needy can sometimes be _____. (1 wd, vs 5)

7. Be very careful not to live as _____; while the wise man sings the foolish man cries. (1 wd, vs 15)

9. Try to understand and do not be a _____ man. (1 wd, vs 17)

114

11. For those who think they can _____, will _____ themselves. (same 1 wd, vs 6)
12. Be careful with your _____, it can be as harmful as smoking. (1 wd, vs 4)
14. Make _____ to the Lord; let the Father be adored. (1 wd, vs 19)

[Puzzle created by Living Word Academy Special Needs Class, Lancaster, Penn.]

Something More to Think About: What do you admire about the Christians you know who know why they believe? Maybe they have studied about the evidence for Jesus' being the Messiah. Or perhaps they know how the Bible was written and planned by God. What thing could you learn to strengthen your faith? Ask a Christian whom you admire for one fact about his or her faith that makes that person strong.

Friday:
You Can Know You're Saved for Sure

Read 1 John 5

Thought for Today: I'm learning that I'm on a rock that I cannot fall off. Regardless of how far I run, I'm still not going to come to the edge of this rock I'm on.... I've learned that God is a rock that we can't fall off.

Steve Mason (Jars of Clay)

Puzzle: Today it's a crossword puzzle! Look up each verse listed to find the word you need to fill in the clue either up and down or from left to right.

1 John 5 Clues:

Across

4. We are God's fans when we carry out his _____. (1 wd, vs 2)

5. If you believe in Jesus Christ, you will ____ eternal life. (1 wd, vs 13)

7. Because I belong to Jesus, this _____ has no hold on me. Through my faith I have been made free. (1 wd, vs 5)

10. Listen to God's wisdom, let's hear it! If you need the _____, try the Holy Spirit. (1 wd, vs 6)

13. If we believe in his Son, _____ we have won. (2 wds, vs 11)

15. When my faith in God helps me through something tough, I'll have _____, even though it's rough. (1 wd, vs 4)

16. Because of our _____ for the Father, we should _____ one another. (same 1 wd, vs 1)

Down

1. I won't call God a _____; my faith keeps my heart on fire. (1 wd, vs 10)

2. Three in one, that much we know, from the Spirit the _____ and water flow. (1 wd, vs 8)

3. God's rules are never _____. When we obey, we put evil on the run. (1 wd, vs 3)

4. Have _____, don't groan. With God you are never alone. (1 wd, vs 14)

6. Some say Jesus is a phony, but the truth is found in God's _____. (1 wd, vs 9)

8. When I _____ by dealing with my fears, I can do anything, even say no to my peers. (1 wd, vs 4)

9. Within _____, God knows best. So ask and trust him for the rest. (2 wds, vs 14)

11. Because I know Jesus in my _____, he and I will never be apart. (1 wd, vs 10)

12. ____ in God's Son and the victory is won. (1 wd, vs 1)

14. Know the _____, know life. No ____, no life. (same 1 wd, vs 12)

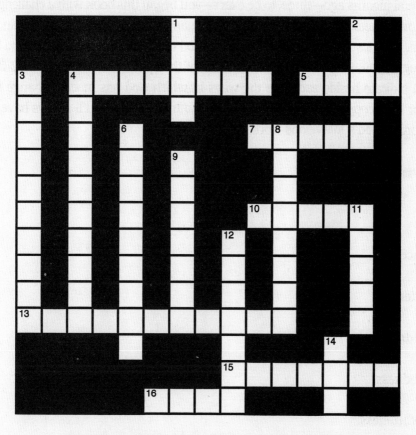

[Puzzle created by Scott Collard and Megan Collard]

Something More to Think About: If you've asked Jesus to come into your life and to be your Savior, think about how God worked to bring you to that point. Did people talk to you about God? Did God make you hungry to know him? Write down as many of these "signs" in your journal as you can.

Weekend Workout:
Inventory Time

Several months ago—three, to be exact—you began this book with a challenge to love others. You've traveled through many puzzles and challenges since then. Now it's inventory time. Since it's good to take notice of the work God is doing in you, look at this list of the fruit of the Spirit from Galatians 5:22-23 and indicate beside each one the ways in which God has made a change in you. Then copy your comments into your journal so that you'll always have a record of God's marvelous work.

Love:

Joy:

Peace:

Patience:

Kindness:

Goodness:

Faithfulness:

Gentleness:

Self-Control:

Don't be discouraged if you are still struggling in areas. God hasn't finished with you yet! Write out in your journal a prayer of praise and thanksgiving for what he's doing in you.

Answer
Key

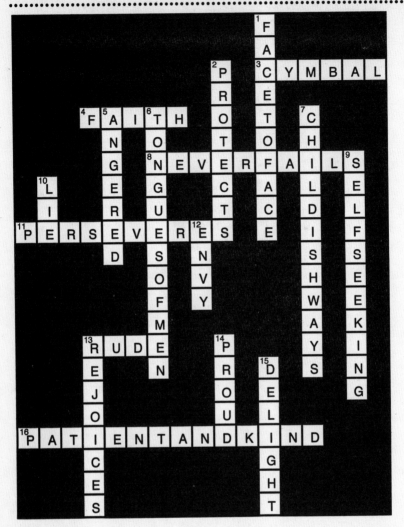

Blessing

Temple porch

Saved

Pity

My spirit

Grain

Great things

Gracious

Northern army

Praise the name

Locusts

Return

Wonders

Elders

Word Find: God is in control.

```
C A A V P R U I M I N P Q T E Q G Y T
F V M U I V M V H H C O O U T V Z W J
A P D G R X I R K B T T K R M C Y I Q
V D C V Z C A O M U L I O N I L M U I
G N O O L B V R U R E E G Y P T O Z E
H U M A N K I N D N E S S A J S F Y P
I V P U K D A A G E M O S T H I G H U
P S A S S Y R I A D Y F R H I W N Q N
O X S W O R D S W I L L F L A S H X P
W F S S H O L Y O N E O S I F B F L E
R U I Z Z X S E A C R V U P V R C I U
Y R O X U A I K D E C E I T W N U F C
F U N W J G U L Q N H O S A A Q J T M
X D O T O Z B O F S A C R I F I C E D
Z L D H P Z U Q O E D S A W L B X D O
C F G P L V E B B J L V E U A H Y D L
G G Z N I A G A P K U I L W I P I Z V
```

1. ISRAEL
2. EGYPT
3. SACRIFICED
4. BURNEDINCENSE
5. HUMANKINDNESS
6. TIESOFLOVE
7. LIFTED
8. ASSYRIA
9. SWORDSWILLFLASH
10. MOSTHIGH
11. COMPASSION
12. HOLYONE

13. AGAIN
14. LION
15. DECEIT

122

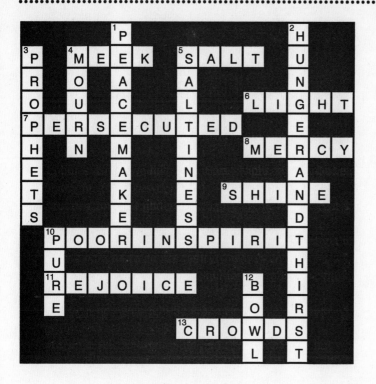

Myrrh

Doves

Pound

Sapphires

Daughters

Garden

Honeycomb

Ivory

Watchmen

Bride

Drink your fill

Heart

Dripped

Cloak

Lebanon

Washed

Beloved

Handles

Polished

Lovely

Perfume

Word Find: Your unconditional love.

```
U  X  E  B  H  Y  T  I  Z  Q  C  B  S  L  Z  J  N  Z  X
J  N  K  G  Z  P  D  L  C  X  U  O  E  L  X  Z  F  A  S
U  Q  N  C  T  M  T  B  R  T  N  T  M  X  O  D  P  A  G
C  I  B  W  X  Z  Z  J  Y  I  V  I  R  D  P  V  B  K  P
D  L  J  N  N  Z  W  T  C  J  G  T  F  D  C  Z  T  F  M
L  E  L  V  V  P  G  G  R  J  P  H  C  X  Y  O  W  N  S
G  F  D  A  A  V  R  N  N  S  M  E  T  J  F  F  V  K  T
T  R  E  A  S  U  R  E  D  P  O  S  S  E  S  S  I  O  N
E  S  L  I  Y  N  E  E  P  Q  P  L  K  T  O  Q  W  T  C
F  Q  I  M  I  O  H  R  M  A  G  I  C  U  S  U  M  H  Y
C  D  G  Q  R  E  F  I  N  E  R  K  D  W  X  G  S  P  H
U  L  H  Q  Y  G  P  H  C  M  M  E  M  F  P  E  F  H  F
T  I  T  Y  N  L  R  W  I  A  P  B  T  N  S  H  H  G  P
E  I  F  I  C  K  I  Z  Y  S  A  Y  R  H  O  R  Z  Y  X
W  X  U  H  P  A  J  L  G  I  C  X  L  A  E  C  L  D  J
J  B  L  G  I  P  N  F  U  K  C  O  M  E  N  W  E  U  G
D  U  L  H  E  R  Z  Y  P  D  E  F  M  B  C  C  A  B  I
I  C  A  C  M  I  K  E  H  R  P  O  K  I  W  D  E  Y  L
Z  D  N  X  I  K  D  O  N  O  T  C  H  A  N  G  E  H  C
E  Z  D  J  E  S  F  U  O  V  A  Z  Q  T  L  G  Y  C  D
P  J  H  J  G  O  Z  B  R  O  B  Y  D  V  M  B  J  E  R
C  E  E  I  N  Z  L  C  V  J  L  T  K  K  T  H  R  N  G
J  S  T  O  R  E  H  O  U  S  E  R  V  E  Y  Z  C  I  U
```

1. PREPARETHEWAY
2. DAYOFHISCOMING
3. REFINER
4. ACCEPTABLE
5. COME
6. DONOTCHANGE
7. ROB

8. TITHES
9. STOREHOUSE
10. PESTS
11. DELIGHTFULLAND
12. SERVE
13. REMEMBRANCE
14. TREASUREDPOSSESSION

15. RIGHTEOUS

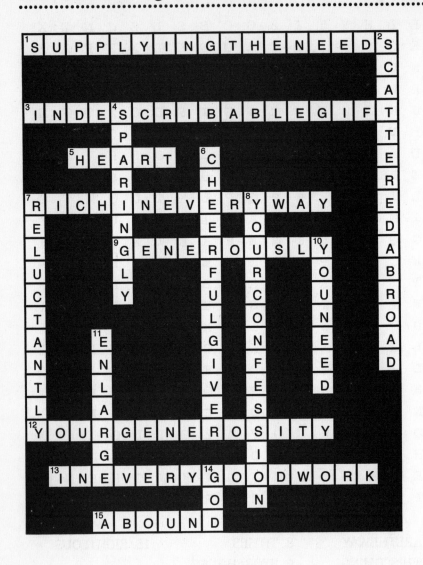

Toils

Listen

Satisfaction

Pleasure

Dreaming

Guard your steps

Heaven

Speech

Rich man

Benefit

Money

Protest

Misfortune

Gladness of heart

Wealth

Word Find: It is never enough.

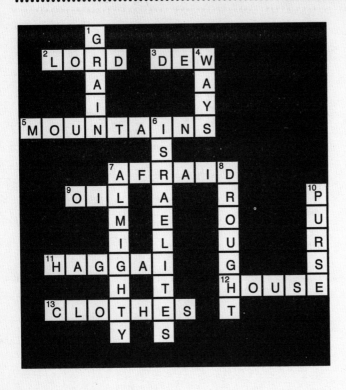

Delighted

Solomon

Mind

Gold

Praise

Attending servants

Talents

Spices

Wisdom

Temple

Cupbearers

Palace

Questions

Queen of Sheba

Word Find: God gives wealth.

Solution to Puzzle Page 36 / Week Three: Monday / Ruth 1

Bethlehem

Judges

Unmarried

Land of Judah

Providing food

Rest

Husbands

Show kindness

Orpah

Wept aloud

Word Find: Being there.

The crossword solution grid reads as follows:

Across:
4. SERVING
6. MANYMEMBERS
7. REVENGE
8. WORSHIP
10. JOYFULINHOPE
11. GOOD
15. FUNCTION
16. GOVERN
18. EVIL
19. HOSPITALITY
22. CONFORM
23. LEADERSHIP
24. BURNINGCOALS

Down:
1. SOBERJUDGMENT
2. PEACE
3. GIVING
5. PROPHESY
9. RENEW
12. GIFTS
13. CONVICTION
14. BEDEVOTED
17. RIGHT
20. LOVE
21. TEACHIN

131

```
D   N   I   A   H   O   C   I   J   E   L   T   O   E
Q   A   J   P   P   L   S   G   A   Q   B   H   G   H
T   C   J   P   A   B   C   N   E   G   R   A   C   E
L   I   K   E   C   F   K   A   P   C   K   N   C   F
U   P   R   A   Y   E   D   M   R   F   B   K   D   D
M   A   G   L   F   D   P   H   I   L   E   M   O   N
R   U   C   G   H   C   F   B   S   I   N   Y   P   B
S   L   A   V   E   H   P   A   O   L   H   G   H   M
D   O   J   B   A   R   C   J   N   Q   L   O   V   E
N   I   B   B   R   O   T   H   E   R   D   D   A   K
E   A   E   M   T   P   I   K   R   L   B   J   O   D
```

1. PAUL

2. PHILEMON

3. GRACE

4. THANK MY GOD

5. PRAY

6. LOVE

7. APPEAL

8. PRISONER

9. HEART

10. SLAVE

11. BROTHER

```
Y R Y V P J P S G S M U O A G U P V N
Q Q H C U T D X O D E Q T A L L U N U
N F H F I R E S T O R E S C U E R G O
F V U B U R F I J D H G Q P R I D E
M Y B C Q S G L R J D Y X J A W F B Z
B F N I T T H A L F F A J H O X Y J R
A P I T G I C P L I H R M I G H T Y T
X F M Y J N K D I L Y R X I Y W H L I
X S H O U T A L O U D O I S R A E L I
M Z G F H H N F N C O G C E Z M L V D
D G L O M E E K S P E A K N O L I E S
C C D P P L A M R P S N T E B R P L M
T B C P E O L A W Y N T O C K A S A B
E R Z R P R M E B K O R U J I S B S Y
K V U E J D K L I I W E R W Z S K Q O
B E E S O L E G B O R W A G A Y E Z G
C E P S H I E X B L O R P Y Q Q T X K
U B Z O B W C G M V N J A T E R X M E
I J Q R K L O G I P G W B I N V N C E
S Y B S Z S J V N F F D N C Q L P X K
```

1. CITYOFOPPRESSORS
2. TRUSTINTHELORD
3. LIONS
4. ARROGANT
5. DOESNOWRONG
6. CUT
7. CITY
8. FIRE
9. PURIFYTHELIPS
10. PRIDE
11. MEEK
12. SPEAKNOLIES
13. SHOUTALOUDOISRAEL
14. MIGHTY
15. RESCUE
16. RESTORE

```
Q K E D K Z A G U E B I W Q H K Q S M
J U V S W C B D H Z T E M P L E N E Z
L H X H Q G S W Q M G F A P I W E K Q
K J L E X Y J O M O D Q I G U M W B M
H L A T W E L V E A N G E L S R H G U
S F M L I J O G A T E S M O A V E E I
M M B Z P A N Q S V F I E R Y L A K E
E U L G E H A V U Q O K I Y M U V E N
A C A E V I A E R H U C L W R S E C W
T J D I V O D A I Q N A B F B C N S J
J I Y Z K W C D N K D C R D E W W L K
Y I H I U K E U G D A F Q E C J G V D
V T R V P N Z S R N T V J C G X K W H
O Z A K C Y T R O Z I H G P V E U K K
A T N Z V S E G D Y O V E R C O M E S
B A A A U U G Z F S N V S O X N M Q E
O D I N E W J E R U S A L E M S T Z R
Q H Q X X G S B Z V R I T I E E R R Z
Q Q L I P J O V B U X Y W I V V G Y W
B M J F S N X S A F I O D F O E I A Q
B L E P L X J A T G F T H R O N E H B
R A R U Z G O L S A O C U B I T S N U
```

1. NEWHEAVEN	8. FIERYLAKE	15. SQUARE
2. NEWJERUSALEM	9. SEVEN	16. CUBITS
3. LIVE	10. GLORY	17. FOUNDATIONS
4. WIPE	11. TWELVEANGELS	18. TEMPLE
5. THRONE	12. GATES	19. NATIONS
6. ALPHAANDTHEOMEGA	13. LAMB	20. IMPURE
7. OVERCOMES	14. MEASURINGROD	

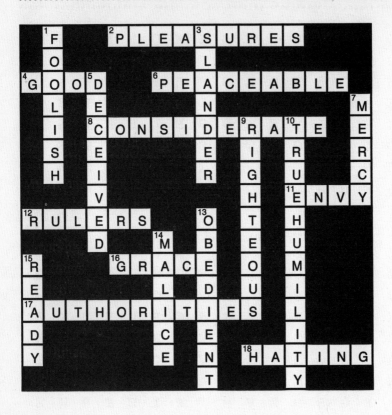

Prisoners

Silver

Sparkle

Consumed

Mouths

Lightning

House

Tribes of Israel

King

Beautiful

Proclaim peace

Ashkelon

Word Find: Read the Bible.

```
F  R  A  R  E  A  D  Y  T  O  C  R  O  S  S  R  N  L  N
V  F  U  L  L  Y  O  B  E  Y  E  D  V  R  S  E  D  L  H
D  Y  W  V  C  Y  N  G  T  O  B  E  A  R  D  P  B  S  K
T  E  R  R  I  T  O  R  Y  M  S  A  I  X  X  W  L  J  P
J  R  S  P  S  I  T  D  P  W  G  M  C  I  A  W  E  H  C
I  J  E  B  H  L  B  E  C  A  R  E  F  U  L  V  B  F  S
A  Z  I  B  Q  F  E  Q  S  D  Y  H  D  Y  R  A  S  Q  S
P  E  M  I  E  G  D  A  Y  D  V  J  M  D  M  X  Q  U  Z
Y  Y  B  X  P  L  I  V  E  S  T  O  C  K  T  V  U  M  O
C  S  U  C  C  E  S  S  F  U  L  N  H  S  O  B  X  D  X
S  V  M  L  Z  C  C  T  R  D  Q  Q  Q  C  S  D  F  P  X
J  U  P  M  H  K  O  D  E  A  T  H  K  R  R  X  Z  P  D
U  U  D  E  H  X  U  U  R  E  K  H  D  J  O  F  R  Q
J  V  X  O  R  E  R  C  R  M  J  L  H  R  X  L  S  B  G
G  G  N  V  U  V  A  L  M  A  O  D  I  A  T  A  C  S  P
K  P  J  U  B  Q  G  R  I  Y  G  J  F  T  K  W  T  E  S
T  K  E  R  O  N  E  V  E  R  L  E  A  V  E  Y  O  U  P
E  K  R  L  V  C  D  F  J  A  Z  B  O  A  D  S  E  P  S
R  C  H  R  D  J  C  S  O  N  O  F  N  U  N  C  B  H  W
N  B  G  Q  Y  R  E  U  B  E  N  I  T  E  S  E  B  R  I
A  V  J  Q  Z  Z  J  X  P  R  R  K  D  F  F  U  L  A  D
I  P  I  P  A  E  Y  O  Z  Y  Z  H  C  H  D  J  L  T  P
C  G  D  B  W  A  J  W  O  O  M  E  D  I  T  A  T  E  S
X  U  I  I  I  N  G  X  K  C  V  J  A  Q  P  N  K  S  E
```

1. DEATH	7. NEVERLEAVEYOU	13. CROSS
2. SONOFNUN	8. COURAGEOUS	14. REUBENITES
3. READYTOCROSS	9. BECAREFUL	15. LIVESTOCK
4. ISRAELITES	10. SUCCESSFUL	16. OCCUPY
5. TERRITORY	11. MEDITATE	17. FULLYOBEYED
6. EUPHRATES	12. DONOTBEDISCOURAGED	18. REBELS

Witchcraft

Assyria

Uproot

Marshal

Destroy

Shepherd

Ruler

Birth

Showers

Origins

Triumph

Invades

Young lion

Carved images

Strongholds

Vengeance

Word Find: From the beginning.

```
M L Z R U D L B M G G U S S I E U A O
C M Y N K W J H T A L B G G X N X Z G
H X T R O X A J S T Q R M H T A X K A
U E F T E N B N H T N E X Z H F L P B
P K D N Q S X D G Y Z S H H A S V J Q
Z N I I X N A R H D T E R N N P C K H
R H U D K F P N U L G E F A K E J H D
M B W L T X P D D B C X A T S A F R T
U Q S E Q G O A T H O N S I N G U O U
D I Z I Q A I D T Z A E A O R V P Y I
G E Y Q U Z N C P C R R G N S S R X U
I Z S M P E T B F O P Z P T T L G E J
S N F C A K E O F D A T E S Q E K C N
G J E C E G D R F X T P W L P M X B M
C S T R E N G T H U M D M Y C W H Y S
O D A Y A Z D K N U I S B B T A M E B
P P H L E F O A R K T D Y P Y B Q W M
Z C U H V L D T N T E P I B Q I N Y I
R N X V U A Z P I T C H E D N C N E F
S N X U X T T R N U S S C Y O H Q V B
U W M Q U W W I F W J M B E B L U F L
M N U T D O O K O T S I Q P F S S D G
Z E G R Y N R L G N Q C Y R M G P U W
R O W L A D L O P Q Y M L R A O W Y G
J B H L O E D L E K P W H A H T F F T
F Y E B F R B E T K S F O N O L G T V
T G O C Y S Y R R X V Z H F U T L C T
P U A P O B M H W M T O E C S Y V Z F
U T D V P E N C H D R I Z B C C S F T
W I G W P J I B S D L L N A I N E S E
```

1. ARK
2. PITCHED
3. FELLOWSHIP
4. CAKEOFDATES
5. APPOINTED
6. PRAISE
7. LYRESANDHARPS
8. TRUMPETS
9. THANKS
10. SING
11. GLORY
12. WONDERS
13. DESCENDANTS
14. OATH
15. LANDOFCANAAN
16. NATION
17. ANOINTED
18. SALVATION
19. IDOLS
20. STRENGTH
21. WORLD
22. FOREST

Gudgodah

Ten commandments

Possess

Buried

Mountain

Covenant

Acacia wood

Forty days and nights

Word Find: Good news.

```
L  H  U  K  Q  O  T  T  H  R  O  W  M  E  H  L  C  Z  N
I  B  N  J  K  Z  N  E  C  A  A  H  G  V  G  U  H  R  H
F  C  S  R  G  R  E  A  T  W  I  N  D  I  J  A  H  O  Y
H  H  H  Q  K  C  I  F  R  O  Y  I  A  M  O  H  I  Y  U
L  G  I  Z  H  E  H  Y  A  R  V  N  T  W  N  N  C  X  R
U  Q  P  H  L  H  R  N  Z  S  U  E  R  M  A  A  N  N  G
N  K  Z  H  Y  O  B  E  H  H  D  V  R  T  H  Y  A  R  V
W  E  F  F  S  Y  E  Z  S  I  Y  A  Y  B  G  X  U  R  C
G  H  C  L  O  X  X  J  I  P  G  H  U  I  O  G  W  A  W
P  D  Y  H  I  O  Y  G  S  T  O  Y  W  S  D  A  X  A  Y
S  B  T  F  J  F  I  S  H  H  V  N  V  H  H  G  R  B  K
E  N  R  Y  X  A  A  N  I  E  U  X  S  A  R  B  E  D  V
L  V  S  T  O  W  G  I  N  L  B  I  C  I  Z  Q  T  A  H
X  F  N  U  C  U  W  J  P  O  E  Y  X  D  B  L  K  X  K
X  W  J  T  H  Y  U  H  H  R  C  C  A  S  T  L  O  T  S
G  W  H  L  K  S  W  U  P  D  E  E  P  S  L  E  E  P  N
C  A  F  S  N  H  W  V  R  C  Z  A  N  H  G  O  Y  Y  O
W  M  K  Q  F  Y  D  W  M  O  P  T  C  T  S  T  U  H  Z
C  W  K  W  O  R  S  X  F  A  E  V  L  H  J  N  R  G  M
```

1. JONAH	9. CASTLOTS
2. NINEVAH	10. RESPONSIBLE
3. PREACH	11. WORSHIPTHELORD
4. RANAWAY	12. THROWME
5. SHIP	13. ROW
6. GREATWIND	14. INNOCENT
7. DEEPSLEEP	15. OVERBOARD
8. GOD	16. FISH

Strengthened

Shattered

Servant

Ahab

Whisper

Cake of bread

Zealous

Covenant

Word Find: The Bible.

145

```
G O T Q J R U Y Z G L V H N J X D I M
W I T S V R A N S C C J Y Z G J I K M
F B H E A H L I R D I I I Q E U I D Z
U Y N E W B O R N B A B I E S O O D L
E M F Q E B Q L I V I N G S T O N E C
I W X A N A T T Y W G K R C G G B Z X
B O C H U A T D U P M Q K G Z E U Z U
R E A R M K O C J U R A N S P K B Y Z
K R A L H Y F A J P E I I E C O W K X
L F M Y B G Q P U D O N E L E Z L P S
H I M F Y P Z S R D F H M S I A S I N
J S D B F S R T R E S P E C T G H R M
X H Z S X A I O K O S J E T G H S X M
V S W Y E M F N S M Y A N I N S O T U
E Q J B B R W E S K W A L Q C V S O S
C C K U E O V V E P R W L C L S Y U D
O X S F T I V A U O J E M R I S I C E
J N F A L Q O B N E E M A W A E J E D
Y U Z D G R S G M T V A G N Y Q L W Z
S V O K J S I F A O S P L G N P C J I
L O M J Z N H G W U T O A I M T R G C
G S G W N P D O E D V S F A E E T B P
G U M E T D I W Q N J T X G C N R W C
J C X J G I Z J I P R E C I O U S C C
Y R B X Y Z U C Y T S Q L A D D H T Y
L P W H I Z P L F C R A G E D J Y D E
M D S V T K H Y Y N M I G A Q H F Q M
J I F P Y L H O A O C J D T W C S Q S
L L N K X H Q Q A C D Q B P M Q A Z B
U H T S X G J E L B M U T S G C R F G
```

1. MALICE	8. ROYAL	15. FEAR
2. NEWBORNBABIES	9. MERCY	16. RESPECT
3. LIVINGSTONE	10. ALIENS	17. BEARSUP
4. HOLYPRIESTHOOD	11. GOODLIVES	18. SUFFERFORDOINGGOOD
5. PRECIOUS	12. SUBMIT	19. EXAMPLE
6. CAPSTONE	13. IGNORANTTALK	20. SINS
7. STUMBLE	14. SERVANTSOFGOD	21. SHEEP

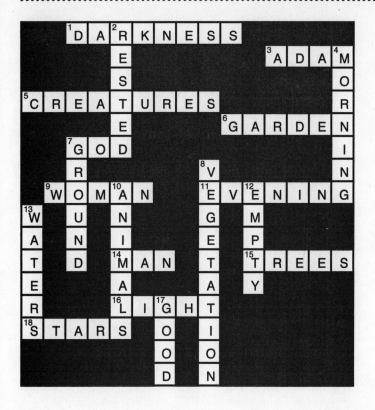

Teaching

Faithless

Gently instruct

Approved

Servant

Quarreling

Godless chatter

Youth

Resurrection

Noble purposes

Devil

Foolish

Stands firm

Instrument

Word Find: He loves you lots.

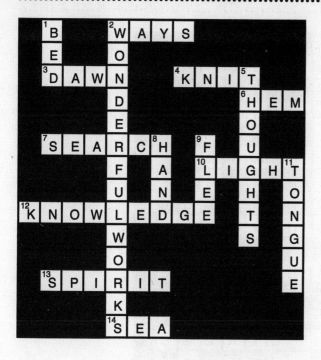

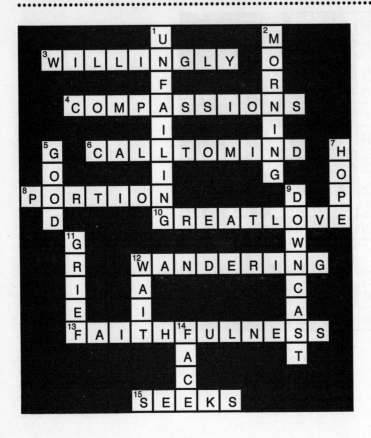

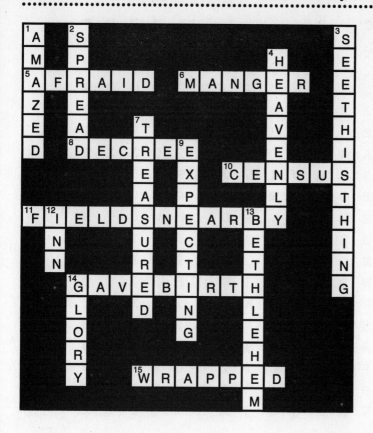

```
E E L Q O Y C J X X L Y R U H B F
J I P H L A R Z F Y E N Y F K R O
U K S O Q X D F D F D X M I G M U
X U W U L H C E Y N D X J D O D N
X H F S F B Q L W S W U S X W D D
B S D E E N B A H N N N V D H B A
P H I V A G I W O A B T I C X X T
S L X E S O M O I L U E R S R D I
B U R N T O F F E R I N G S O G O
W E P T E D U M Y S L A M W G T N
Q I P H U Z P O R O D M F J P I S
I Y P M N O I S E Q T P P O R S S
H H M O N E Y E F H H M F B I Q Q
G K O N F X I S R A E L I T E S T
V P G T S R G F J I A P E Q S V X
M D Q H A F L B N S L E V I T E S
E E A I P D I R J Y T C G F S P M
C X U S B Y W L P B A I N O E I Q
Z H G K V K P Q S Q R K M Q F Q E
```

1. ISRAELITES
2. BUILDTHEALTAR
3. LAWOFMOSES
4. BURNTOFFERINGS
5. FOUNDATION
6. FEAST
7. SEVENTHMONTH
8. MONEY
9. OIL
10. LEVITES
11. HOUSE
12. PRIESTS
13. GOOD
14. WEPT
15. NOISE

1 GRACIOUS
2 GOVERNORS
3 VERYMUCHAFRAID
4 SADNESSOFHEART
5 CUPBEARER
6 PRAYED
7 JERUSALEM
8 BACK
9 AWESOME
10 SINS
11 KINGSFOREST
12 BURNED
13 SUCCESS
14 FAVOR
15 MOURNED
16 JUDAH

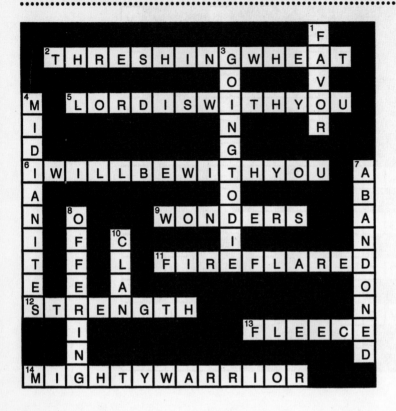

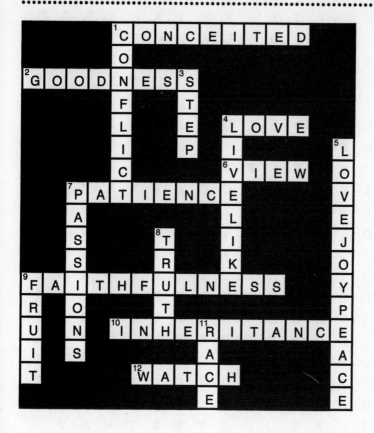

```
J E J M K C I J F P X W T X O Y K A Q
K I N E I H X L O A L A K G E K D U G
I S U B A T C O N S E C R A T E G A Y
Q Q P T H L M A N M H D J H N L T T D
J O N U I N O L S N E U N I T D V K M
N R O D L F S U B I U M A N N A A Z I
B J Q B M P E B S T T L W X T D Y L M
J A J D C V S E S F P L O J E A G U I
M K J D I Y H Z N M O S E V E N T Y Z
F A L G R P Z Y O L Z R Y W O D B D C
C J S E O Q C C E X V S M M G M E N H
U Q M R J I W H W X X P A Y Q E E W I
P I P F J Y Q X H X I D L U S D M H E
F Z A R L O E O Q J E M O R R A C O E
R M L R I V A L S N H Y E U O D K L T
Z Y A W Q D N R R E H D B W D U B E X
E R C H D N E U Y T N S U V E B C M F
Y Z E L S B B L I A O I Q C A R C O F
D Y G O M K C W I G L O Z R K H S N M
H G I U S O K R D F F T H E T E N T T
Q K C T P A O S Y Z L T K E K O W H P
N U R S E C A R R I E S E A A F L X L
C A M P A T N I G H T T C M Q V V B L
O R S N X M W F X G Y O I N C D Y M B
```

1. COMPLAINED	9. MOSES	17. WHOLEMONTH
2. BURNEDAMONG	10. BURDEN	18. THETENT
3. RABBLE	11. NURSECARRIES	19. PROPHESIED
4. CUCUMBERS	12. GIVEUSMEAT	20. ELDADANDMEDAD
5. MANNA	13. TOOHEAVY	21. JOSHUA
6. CORIANDERSEED	14. SEVENTY	22. JEALOUSFORMYSAKE
7. CAKES	15. SPEAKWITHYOU	23. TEETH
8. CAMPATNIGHT	16. CONSECRATE	

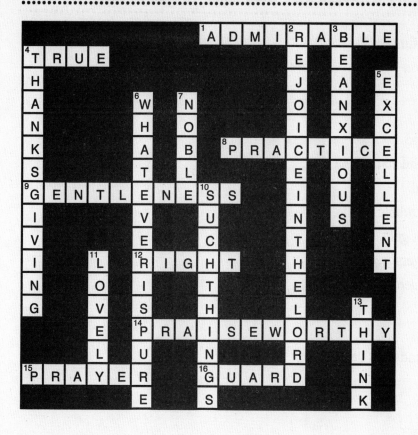

Blazing furnace

Dedication

Soldiers

Trusted

Abednego

King Nebuchadnezzar

Scorched

Piles of rubble

Image of gold

Astrologers

Amazement

Rescue

Word Find: It is bad for me.

```
F X C E C H Q A V X M G A R N K H T S
R M M Q U V H D W U A P F O A X S N A
T T R U M P E T S H K W R W I E G G U
Y U H B O E F V C I F R A L U F T T Y
W T B R M P A S Z U Y B I V W F A V E
H O U S E O F A B I N A D A B L D Q A
K A R N B S A C Y Z G T W R A T H U N
O F N W I U H R B G I P B K V W G B S
D H T E N T O I F I G U W O H J P G C
I Q O I K F L F N P D M L F U K X D U
L F F W A L K I N G M H O G M G P H T
B Y F M V B N C J U F T A O P R Q V U
N B E Z I H B E P O A L F D W D N K X
H S R I T C A D C I T Y O F D A V I D
J Q I W D T H A G G O L F O P Q N D J
W Y N R V L K A N G E R B U R N E D N
X W G C E I Z B L X N K R L T N K P R
D N S E S R D L I N E N E P H O D V U
R A H Y X L G E U X U S A P S X W B H
T M B Y H O U S E H O L D A K T M Z S
W W I I G N D S X N I W H R D M K X M
H O B H M B H E P N C G W A N O M X W
D A V I D W A D H O L L N T H Z C U H
```

1. DAVID
2. ARKOFGOD
3. HOUSEOFABINADAB
4. WALKING
5. THRESHINGFLOOR
6. ANGERBURNED
7. WRATH
8. AFRAID
9. CITYOFDAVID
10. HOUSEHOLD
11. BLESSED
12. SACRIFICED
13. LINENEPHOD
14. TRUMPETS
15. MICHAL
16. TENT
17. BURNTOFFERINGS
18. LOAFOFBREAD

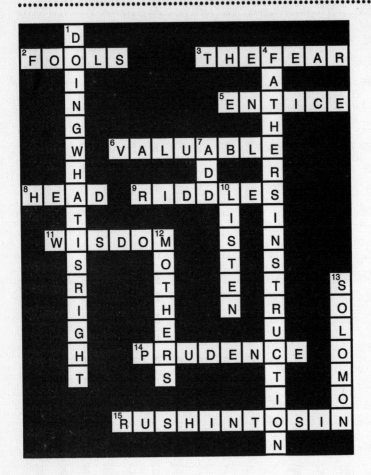

160

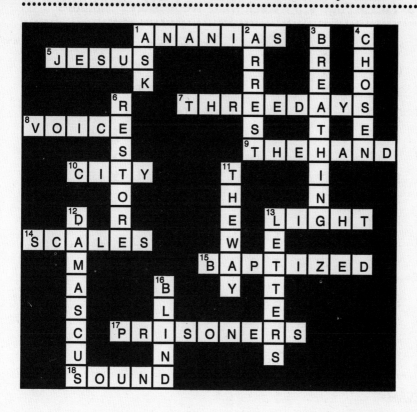

```
        C  S  A              H  T  Q
     F  Q  S  W  W           B  E  H  R  I
  G  Y  P  L  O  T           F  E  E  T  F  K
T  I  N  U  O  J  H  W     V  Z  X  L  C  V  S  N
R  O  I  P  W  U  Y  H  S  N  M  Y  O  K  E  B  B
E  R  N  T  T  G  F  D  S  A  R  Z  R  X  C  V  Y
T  H  E  L  O  R  D  I  S  G  O  O  D  P  L  M  H
   S  V  E  A  W  Q  A  S  Y  C  U  I  O  N  U
      A  Z  N  X  C  V  F  B  K  U  J  H  P
      H  A  G  S  E  R  O  Q  S  Q  G  Y  O
      R  E  B  U  K  E  S  I  O  J  P
      R  A  W  E  S  T  P  H  J
         V  S  F  C  X
         C  N  C
         X
```

1. NINEVAH
2. THELORD
3. SLOWTOANGER
4. REBUKES
5. ROCKS
6. THELORDISGOOD
7. FOES
8. PLOT
9. YOKE
10. FEET

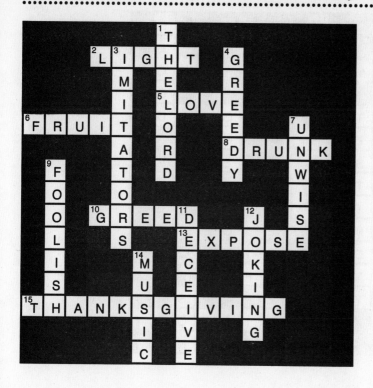